THE SCIENCE OF LUCK

THE SCIENCE OF LUCK

INSIGHTS FROM PSYCHOLOGY, ECONOMICS, PHILOSOPHY AND ENTREPRENEURSHIP

Moh Hon Meng

ISBN: 1546594604
ISBN-13: 9781546594604
Library of Congress Control Number: 2017907646
CreateSpace Independent Publishing Platform
North Charleston, South Carolina

For all the people working in the companies I cofounded and invested in, who are battling with luck on a daily basis.

CONTENT

INTRODUCTION

Swimming in the clear waters of Boracay in the Philippines and looking at an amazing sunset over the horizon of the Sulu Sea, I wondered how ancient humans must have thought about the sun. What an awesome and mysterious thing the sun is!

Of course, it was not possible for early humans to know about the sun. So what most cultures did was think of it as a god. The sun is a powerful thing that lights up the sky and gives warmth. It must be a god.

And so it went with many other things humans did not understand. Why do the rains come regularly most years but not others? There must be a god in control of the rains, and he must be withholding it when he is displeased. Oh, what scary and amazing things are lightning and thunder! What power! There must be a lightning god who controls it. As a race, we basically invented gods for everything we did not understand.

There were the Egyptian gods, the Roman gods, the Greek gods, the Viking gods, the Chinese mystical gods, and lots of other gods from ancient cultures. They all had gods who were in charge of various kinds of natural phenomenon.

We also created gods for personal matters. There were gods who were in charge of love, of success and fortune, of studiousness and intelligence, and many other factors. Why is that one person always successful in his hunt? Why is it that so many men fall in love with her? Why does she understand the problems so much quicker than everyone else? It was near impossible to explain these things; it must have been the work of gods who favored one individual over another and perhaps even counseled him or her on a daily basis. The gods could even have been at work in manipulating our minds and emotions as it pleased them to achieve their ends.

Those were the nice things. The flip side was tragic. The people who were born with mental disabilities such as Down syndrome and autism or who developed dementia and schizophrenia later in life were thought to be cursed by the gods or possessed by demons. These people were condemned, banished, and destroyed. To ease our guilt and our feelings of ignorance and helplessness, we created priests who told us that it was the will of the gods, and since the gods willed it, we could only obey.

As human beings gained more and more understanding about how the universe works, many cultures started doing away with the multitude of gods. We now know what the sun is, so there is no need to worship it as a god. We now know what accounts for the unpredictability of the rains, so there is no need to give sacrifices to the rain god. We now know what lightning and thunder are, so we have turned the lightning god into a comic book superhero instead.

In personal matters also, we have gained tremendous knowledge. We now know that Down syndrome, schizophrenia, and dementia are conditions of the brain, so we no longer think of them as demon possessions.

We also understand how interpersonal attraction works, so we have *mostly* given up on the love gods. We now know, scientifically, that there are ways in which a person can make himself or herself more attractive to potential mates, so there's knowledge we can act on. But we've not completely given up on the love gods yet because love is special! We might have all the scientific reasons for why love happens, but it's still magical when it does, so we still put Venus, Cupid, the Sandman, and other love deities into our books and songs, but we don't really believe that it is their work.

So what is luck?

Luck is a little like love! It's magical when it happens. There we are, doing our own thing, and then seemingly out of nowhere, something good happens that changes our lives for the better! We giggle like crazy, and we experience a kind of warmth that's like the gods wrapping their arms around us. Bad luck is the opposite. It feels like the whole world has abandoned us. We instinctively think back to all the sins we've committed and wonder if the gods are punishing us.

We look at the luck around us and wonder, Why is it that some people always seem to get the best things in life, and others can never get a break? It all seems so random and hard to explain. It must be the work of Fortuna, the Roman goddess of luck and fate, or Cai Shen Ye, the Chinese god of fortune. They must be the ones who make the decisions to give out more success to some and less to others. But as with the sun and the rain and love, it is not the work of the gods. There are ways to describe luck in a rational manner.

To start, let's define "luck": *luck is simply unexpected good things or the absence of bad things happening to us.*

"Good things" could be assistance, rewards, opportunities, extra time—basically extra resources of all kinds that improve our lives. "Bad things" could be problems, obstacles, challenges, bad relationships—anything that makes life difficult for us.

So when we wish someone good luck, we are saying, "Over and above the plans you have made, I wish for you to receive unexpected additional resources that will help you achieve your goals faster and easier and experience a journey that is unexpectedly absent of obstacles and difficulties."

The issue is with the word "unexpected." How do we describe something that is unexpected? If we can describe it, doesn't it become expected?

Yes, it does!

When we don't understand how luck works and we get additional resources that help us, we will be very surprised. It will seem like divine intervention. But when we know how luck works, we can create the situations where luck is likely to happen and *expect* our lucky breaks!

At university I studied psychology, economics, and philosophy. Those were subjects I loved, and I've kept up with the developments in those disciplines over the years. I've always tried to apply the things I've learned in my own life and observe them as they are applied by others. Since graduation, I've largely been an Internet entrepreneur. I made my pot of gold in an early venture, and I've since cofounded and invested in several other businesses. I've experienced luck personally on many occasions, and I've seen it happen to other people as well.

It is from the perspective of the three subjects I studied at university and my own business experience that I write this book on luck. I've titled it *The Science of Luck* to communicate that I'm going to approach the subject factually and logically. Luck cannot be a science in the way that chemistry is a science. But it qualifies as a social science because what we call luck is really a mixture of several subjects of study about the human condition.

Luck is economical and mathematical. We have to know about probabilities, costs, and benefits and how to bet and invest in ways that will maximize our returns. Luck is psychological and sociological. There's a lot of it that is grounded in behavioral conditioning, social upbringing, and cognitive perception; there are biases, misattributions, and triggers. And luck is philosophical. There are logical fallacies, superstitious practices, and cultural and religious beliefs surrounding it.

To make the book easier to read and understand, I won't be dryly describing the science behind luck. Instead, I'll mainly be using stories to illustrate the points. I'll also be sharing stories from my own experiences. I think businesspeople experience luck the most (both good and bad) and so are filled with experiences to share. We start out thinking it is our own cleverness that makes us successful. But as we age and look back, we realize luck had a huge role to play. I can see *how and why luck happened*, and I can see the things that *led up to it*, so that's what I'll be sharing in this book.

At the end of this book, you should be able to do the following:

1. Recognize the situations where good luck happens and what to do about them.
2. Know your luck situation and how to improve it.

3. Know the skills and character traits required to increase the odds of good luck.
4. Understand the superstitions that people have about luck and how to use them correctly.
5. Improve your timing for good luck.
6. Increase your awareness of the things happening around you that contribute to luck.
7. Handle good and bad luck when they come.

This book is for everyone who is *striving* to achieve success. It is not for the person who just wants to hit the lottery. In fact, in the chapter called "Lottery Luck," I point out that playing the lottery is one of the worst things for anyone to do.

If you're willing to work hard to make your life better, this book will increase your understanding of the principles that lead to good luck. If you are determined to put them into practice, your luck will improve significantly!

Let your journey of great luck begin!

PART I

LUCK BASICS

THE SINGLE MOST IMPORTANT THING
ABOUT LUCK: POSITIVE ENERGY

Energy and persistence conquer all things.

—BENJAMIN FRANKLIN

WHAT CREATED THE universe?

On a website called Universe Forum (which is produced for NASA by the Harvard Smithsonian Center for Astrophysics), I spotted a small paragraph that says this:

> *The leading idea is called the "inflationary universe" model. The key assumption of this model is that just before the Big Bang, space was filled with an unstable form of energy, whose nature is not yet known. At some instant, this energy was transformed into the fundamental particles from which arose all the matter we observe today. That instant marks what we call the Big Bang.*

So before the beginning, there was simply energy. And that energy later transformed into all the matter in the universe. Everything we see around us, *including ourselves,* is formed from energy.

When I googled "the most important qualities for success," the top posts listed items like "drive," "passion," "willpower," and "persistence." This is *human* energy expressed in different words.

Now, hold on; you might be thinking, Is this guy equating energy as it is understood in physics with the energy we have as humans? Yes, I am!

If you google "what is energy in physics," the answer you will get is simply "the ability to get work done." The various words we use to describe energy in physics, such as "kinetic," "gravitational," and "electrical," among many others, are *not* different types of energy. They are one universal energy in different forms. Humans have invented different words to differentiate the forms, but we mustn't let these words fragment our understanding of the universe. The Law of Conservation of Energy tells us that all the energy in the universe is constant. Energy cannot be created or destroyed. It simply converts from one form to another.

If energy cannot be created but only transformed, where does the energy I have when I move a rock from point A to point B come from? It comes from the food matter that my body has broken down through the process of digestion into the fuel called glucose. Where does the food matter come from? It comes from plants that have absorbed energy from the sun and created food for itself through the process of photosynthesis. Where does the sun's energy come from? It comes from its own mass and the process of fusion. Where does the sun's mass come from? If we keep asking this line of questions, we go all the way back to the Big Bang.

Now, besides moving a rock from point A to point B, I also use energy to meet people, talk to them, and persuade them to my ideas. And then maybe together we decide to move a bunch of rocks and create a house. And then after that maybe more people decide to build houses and a city appears.

Human energy is a form of universal energy. We use that energy to act on the universe—setting things in motion, putting things together, breaking things apart—and we transform the universe in ways big and small.

POSITIVE ENERGY

We can use the energy we have for destructive purposes or creative purposes; we can make stuff or break stuff, much like what the universe does. So I make a distinction here and call energy that is devoted to creating stuff Positive Energy and the energy that is devoted to breaking stuff Negative Energy.

Positive Energy is good, optimistic, and happy. It always regards things as possible rather than impossible; it is engaging and seeks to connect people and things rather than set them apart. It is true, honest, and authentic. It is ever open and ready to receive things that help with the creative process. It makes things move, grow, and succeed!

Negative Energy is destructive and angry. It focuses on the downside of things and is always distrustful, hateful, and skeptical. It tears down social connections and seeks personal gratification and gain. It is fake, deceitful and manipulative.

Why would human beings use the energy they have for negative things? There are many reasons. Sometimes a person thinks that there is personal gain to be had when a project fails, so he devotes his energy towards destroying the project. Sometimes a person wants revenge for real or perceived offenses that he has received from others. Sometimes a person just wants to demonstrate power and influence to satisfy his own ego. Although a person may stand to gain some advantage in the short term from using Negative Energy, he will attract bad luck and misery in the long run.

Another state of being is Non Energy, where we don't devote the energy we have to creative or destructive things. We simply float along in life, using our energy to consume things, do as we are told, and take things as they come along. We do not conceive ideas and push for them to happen. It is perfectly fine to stay in this state if you are happy with it.

But if you want to make something good happen, if you want *your* ideas to happen, you need Positive Energy.

A POSITIVE ENERGY STORY

A young man with tremendous Positive Energy came across two scrawny potatoes along the road to the village. He picked them up and said, "What luck! I am going to make potato soup. Yes, I'm going to make the best potato soup ever! It's going to be the king of potato soups! King Potato Soup!"

As he walked happily along his path, he told everyone he met about the great luck he'd had that day and how the King Potato Soup was going to be the most wondrous soup anyone had ever seen. He talked about how amazing the soup would taste and smell and how loads of people would come from afar to try it.

An old woodcutter was curious about the soup and told the young man, "I don't know about cooking great soup, but I do know about the cleanest, freshest water that anyone has ever tasted. It's up by the hill, flowing down a stream. I think your soup should use that water."

The young man said, "Really! That is so wonderful! Can you show me where it is?"

The old woodcutter replied, "Sure, but I want a bowl of that King Potato Soup that you are cooking. Would that be all right?"

The young man said, "That would be more than all right! That would be super!"

So the woodcutter showed the young man the stream, and the two of them carried buckets full of the cleanest, freshest water and loaded them onto the woodcutter's donkey. Then they both walked on the path toward the village.

Unknown to them, a woman who made pots for a living was waiting for them. She had heard about the King Potato Soup from passersby, and she had some old pots in her home she was hoping she could exchange for some of that amazing soup.

When the young man and the woodcutter reached her house, she ran out to meet them and said, "Hey, I heard about the King Potato Soup. I've never seen or heard of something like that before, but it sure sounds tasty. I have some old cooking pots in the back. Can I loan them to you in exchange for some of that soup?"

The young man said, "That would be super! I think we will cook the soup right here!"

So they set up the pots and poured in the water from the stream, and the woodcutter put some firewood underneath the pot and asked, "Do we start cooking now?"

The young man said, "Oh no, it's just the three of us. A lot more people should know about this soup. I'll go to town to tell them about it. Wait for me. I'll be back."

So the young man continued on his path and met a great number of people. Some of them had already heard about the soup, and others were hearing about it for the first time from the young man. Many people wanted a share of the soup, and they offered things they had in exchange. Carrots, onions, salt—the list of ingredients went on.

And then the young man met a potato farmer who said, "I heard about your great potato soup, and you probably have a lot of potatoes, but I'm a potato farmer, and all I have are potatoes. I was wondering if I could give you some in exchange for a bit of that great soup you are cooking."

The young man said, "That would be super!"

Along the way, the young man also met many chefs who told him they had tasted the King Potato Soup before from lands far away and that they each had a special twist to the recipe. They asked if they could help cook the soup in exchange for a bowl of it.

"That would be super!" the young man said.

So the young man went back to the pot maker's home with many people and many things. The chefs helped with the cooking, and all those with ingredients threw them into the pots according to the chefs' instructions, and they cooked many pots of amazing soup.

When it was done, they all sat around the warmth of the pots and ate the best soup they had ever had.

And when the young man sat to enjoy his bowl of King Potato Soup, he said to himself, "What a lucky day! I was so lucky to find the potatoes and so lucky to meet all these wonderful people who helped to make the soup! I am such a lucky guy!"

A NEGATIVE ENERGY STORY

A young man with Negative Energy came across two scrawny potatoes along the road to the village. He kicked them aside angrily and said, "What terrible luck! I can't even find potatoes that are sizable enough to fill my stomach."

End of story.

YES, IT HAPPENS!

Does my Positive Energy story sound too good to be true? It's not. I've seen it happen many times. I have an idea that I think is exciting, and I start working on it and tell others about it. Soon I get calls from colleagues, bosses, friends, and even strangers saying, "Hey, your project looks interesting. Can I join you? I have skills I think you might need."

Then word spreads that a team of people is working on a project, and then maybe the project gets featured in the company newsletter, or better still a journalist writes about it in the local newspaper because he thinks it makes an interesting story, and we get more calls from people who want to help us and join us.

That is luck! It is "unexpected resources" that come out of nowhere. When I was younger, I did not plan for this unexpected external help. How could I say, "We'll just wait for unexpected assistance to appear"? I couldn't and didn't. So when the offers of help came, it felt like they came out of the blue, like I was especially loved by some higher power who had directed them to me! But having experienced it many times now, I can say that it's to be expected. *If you start something meaningful and put lots of Positive Energy behind it, others will join you and help you.*

I've been on the other side as well and become other people's unexpected assistance and opportunity. I have approached acquaintances and complete strangers and offered to help in one way or another simply because I liked the activity they were doing. Some of them did not know I existed or that I would help in the ways I did. But they were doing something worthwhile, and I wanted to be a part.

When I work with young entrepreneurs, I see people with Positive and Negative Energy clearly. The Positive Energy ones are always happy, smiling, and excited, and they are sharing their ideas with everyone and getting advice and feedback and offers of help. I am always happy to interact with them and share my experience and contacts, even if I don't have a personal stake in their ventures.

The Negative Energy ones are closed, secretive, distrustful of everyone, and have only bad things to say about the people they meet. They whine and complain about everything. I don't even want to listen to their ideas because they will never get it off the ground. There's no point wasting my time on them.

WHY DOES THIS WORK?

It works because *human beings have a need to believe that life will become better.* We are a species that is constantly evolving. If we do not believe life will be better, we will not evolve.

"Go to the moon? Stupid idea, it will never work."

"Eradicate smallpox? It's impossible."

"Connect everyone on Earth? You must be dreaming."

We've heard the negativism before. In anything that people want to do, there are always the Negative Energy naysayers who kick the idea to the side of the road and say it is the dumbest idea they've ever heard.

But there will be the Positive Energy go-getters who say, "I think it's possible." And they come together to work on the idea and attract people with talents and other resources to join them. In the end, they go on to improve the world, in big ways and small, and they advance the human race.

Some fail, of course. But if they put good, honest energy behind their efforts, their failures will not be total losses because they will have learned important lessons for their future projects. Their failure may even be useful to those who attempt the same idea later because they can try new approaches.

Human beings want to believe life will be better tomorrow than it is today. When I phrase this more personally, it becomes: I want tomorrow to be better than it is today. And you want tomorrow to be better than it is today.

Because we all want tomorrow to be better than today, we find ideas and people that have the potential to improve our lives very attractive. It makes us want to contribute our time, effort and resources to help make them succeed. And because our collective experience as a race has been that good things don't come easily, we are able to persevere in our work and support of good ideas and people despite great hardships.

We want to believe we will be able to overcome all odds to achieve the kinds of things we want to achieve. *It is an evolutionary impulse that has given us a unique and powerful advantage over all the other animals.*

That's why Positive Energy that seeks to create and build resonates powerfully with people. If you are the person with the Positive Energy and the ideas, people will emerge from places you did not expect to *give you* what they have to help you succeed. That is *luck*!

RICH HABITS

Thomas C. Corley, who did a five year interview with 233 millionaires and authored the book *Change Your Habits, Change Your Life*, wrote an article for the *BusinessInsider* website on 13 February 2016, where he says

> *Luck hides inside positivity. Opportunities have to be seen in order to be embraced. Positivity opens the mind to opportunities. Positivity means having a positive mental outlook. It is the springboard of all creativity and insight.*
>
> *Problem solving requires creativity and insight, and self-made millionaires are, by default, problem-solvers. Their optimistic outlook enables them to see possibilities for solutions. Positivity also creates a higher level of confidence and an expectation that good things will happen. Positivity is the fertilizer in which good luck grows.*

I recommend reading the book *Change Your Habits, Change Your Life*. It will give you insights into how successful people think and live. You may be surprised that real millionaires are not like how they are depicted in the movies. For example, Corley says

> *64% of them own modest homes. They've owned their home for at least 20 years. Very few of them get divorced. They drive old cars. They hardly ever lease a car. 96% of them spend less than $6,000 a year on vacations. 41% of them spend less than $3,000 a year.*

Part of the reasons the millionaires that Corley interviewed are successful is that they work very hard at their jobs or businesses, and they are very frugal with their money. I've read books like this early on in my career (another good one is *The Millionaire Next Door* by Thomas J. Stanley), and they have given me the right mental picture of what successful people are like, replacing the wrong mental picture of rich people that the media places in our minds all the time. This has helped me envision my life and the route I should take.

CULTIVATING POSITIVE ENERGY

If you are not someone with a lot of Positive Energy, here are some tips gathered from the field of positive psychology and my own experience:

1. CHECK YOUR OWN NEGATIVISM

It is easy to recognize negativism in other people, but can you recognize the negativism in yourself? Here are the top tips:

Stop Complaining. Don't complain about anything, big or small. Someone gave you a dirty look, a service staff was rude to you, your boss scolded you in front of everyone—it doesn't matter. When you complain about things, you are in fact giving energy to the complaints, which makes the situation worse. If you learn to stop complaining, you will realize that many of the things you currently complain about are really very trivial, and they will stop having any effect on you.

For the important things, focus on the solution to your problem instead of dwelling on how unfair the whole situation is to you. When you do that, you exert energy toward the solution and the positive outcome. You'll feel more constructive, and you'll eventually work out a solution.

Stop cussing. Why is there a need to swear and cuss at all? When you cuss, you add Negative Energy to your situation.

Stop worrying. Don't give energy to your worries. Again, focus on finding the solution to your problem.

Stop your own drama. Do you often feel offended? If you do, you will feel entitled to a response to your feelings of being offended, and you will start devoting energy to seeking emotional satisfaction from the people you think caused you the offense. When you do that, you are giving energy to your negative emotions, and you will drag other people in to satisfy those emotions and make things worse.

2. BUILD YOUR OWN POSITIVE ENERGY

Smile. Do you think people smile because they are happy or that they become happy when they smile? Research in psychology tells us that it is both. So smile often, and you will be happier and project Positive Energy.

Compliment. The basis of this is really about developing an appreciative mind that spots the good in people and things. Giving a compliment is the projection of that appreciative mind-set. When you have that mind-set, you will see possibilities instead of obstacles. Now, do you compliment because you have an appreciative mind-set or do you develop an appreciative mind-set because you compliment? Again, it is both.

Start exercising. Read the chapter called "The Temple of Luck." To have Positive Energy, you need physical energy and stamina, and that comes from taking care of your body.

See the bright side. There is always a bright side. There is always something you can work on constructively. Focus on that, and give energy to that. Do not dwell on your thoughts of unfairness, worry, offense, or anything else that is negative. Do not give energy to those negative emotions to grow.

3. HANG WITH POSITIVE ENERGY PEOPLE

<u>Your peers.</u> Hang with those with tremendous Positive Energy in school. These are the people who will become important later in life. When they do, you might need their help. I find that people have tremendous affection for those they went to school with. There's a high level of familiarity and trust that is difficult to develop after school. So you want to invest in Positive Energy relationships early on if you can.

<u>Your colleagues.</u> Hang with those who are driven and want to get things done. There will always be an opposing group who will complain about the Positive Energy group, make sarcastic remarks about them, and try to appear cool while doing so. Avoid this group like they are people with infectious diseases.

<u>Your seniors and bosses.</u> Volunteer for all projects that will get you in contact with bosses and seniors who have Positive Energy. You may find there are good opportunities to do so. For example, your company might start a cross-departmental committee to plan the annual dinner and dance or company run. Volunteer for these to network with others, showcase your abilities to a larger group of people across the company, and learn from high-energy seniors and bosses.

<u>It's high-energy people, not rich or powerful people.</u> Some people think that as long as they hang with people who are rich and powerful, they will get some benefits. That may not be true if the rich or powerful people have low energy. They may be at the stage in their lives where they don't really want to do much but just enjoy the fruits of what they have already achieved. Of course, rich and powerful people who are still full of energy are full of possibilities. Hang with them if you can.

4. AVOID NEGATIVE ENERGY PEOPLE

Avoid people with Negative Energy. They are the ones with constant worries, endless complaints, tiresome emotional drama, continuous constant offense, and secretive defensiveness. If you hang with them, you will waste a lot of energy managing their issues.

5. GET INVOLVED IN WHAT'S NEW

What is new has a lot of Positive Energy. If your company is launching a major new product or business division, try to get involved. Such projects usually have a lot of resources, support, and visibility. The whole company will be looking for the project to succeed. When it does, there will be plenty of opportunities for rewards and promotions.

If you look at it from a higher level, you will see that the world also has new things it gets into all the time: new inventions are created, new trends get started, and new discoveries are made. You can think about how to get involved in these new things too.

SCIENCE

The science that I've drawn from in this chapter includes physics, evolution, and positive psychology.

The universe was created with energy, and you control a part of that energy. What you do with it affects your life and the lives of others around you. Use it positively, and you will tap into the human race's need to evolve and become better, and you will receive unexpected help. Use it negatively, and you will repel people.

Use the tips from positive psychology to develop Positive Energy. You will attract others to you, and they will help you. That's when good luck will find you!

Luck comes from Positive Energy.

WHAT DO YOU WANT LUCK FOR?

*Luck is everything. My good luck in life was to be
a really frightened person. I'm fortunate to be a
coward, to have a low threshold of fear, because
a hero couldn't make a good suspense film.*

—ALFRED HITCHCOCK

IF YOU SAY you want to win the lottery, you can put this book down right
now and walk away. In the chapter called "Lottery Luck," I talk about
why trying to win the lottery is one of the worst things you can do. I've
seen people devote a lot of energy to the lottery, but it's a waste of life.

My question is, What is it that you want to do with your life?

There are no fairy godmothers, but there are millionaires and bil-
lionaires and people in positions of power and influence whom you may
come across in your life who can and want to help you achieve what you
are after. When your paths cross, what will you tell them?

If you don't know what you want, you could have great luck hitting
you in the face every day, and you wouldn't notice it.

WHEN LUCK COMES KNOCKING AND YOU'RE NOT HOME

Not long ago, I met a young man at an entrepreneurship seminar who
was quite rude. He was graduating from university, and it was pure
chance that we ended up talking to each other at the seminar. He had

tremendous energy, but he used it to go on and on about everything that was wrong with the world.

A year later, he called me, told me he was selling cars, and asked if I was in the market to buy one. Having felt the brunt of his Negative Energy, I turned him down, even though I was indeed looking to buy a car.

So when this young man was talking to me at the seminar, who was I to him? *I could have been a number of things that he wanted me to be.* I could have been a potential investor in his business if he had an idea for one. I could have been a powerful referrer to a job in an industry he really wanted to get into. I could have been a mentor and given him some valuable advice. As it turned out, I could have bought a car from him and introduced him to people who were also looking to buy cars.

I could have been the god of luck sent by fate, escorted by the gods of fortune and happiness.

But I turned out to be nothing for this young man. It was his Negative Energy, yes, but it stemmed from him not knowing what he wanted to do with his life. *If he had had a clear idea, he would have known how to place me the moment he met me*, and he would have proceeded to interact with me in a way that helped him achieve what he wanted. But because he didn't know what he wanted, the meeting with me turned out to be a waste of time for the both of us.

DO WE ALL KNOW WHAT WE WANT?

I don't want to make it seem as though everyone knows what they want early in life. With the story above, I am really making a couple of points, and I do generally go easy on young people!

I think some people are lucky, and they know what they want to do with their lives early on. But most people don't, and they try different things before deciding. Even then, it can change as life goes on because people's priorities and perspectives about life change as they gain more experience.

The people who do know what they want are amazing when we meet them. We are envious of their clarity and how much energy they are already putting into their goals.

Those of us who are entrepreneurs love to invoke Steve Jobs, the cofounder of Apple and Pixar. This is a speech he made at a commencement address he gave on June 12, 2005 at Stanford University.

I was lucky—I found what I loved to do early in life...Sometimes life hits you in the head with a brick. Don't lose faith. I'm convinced that the only thing that kept me going was that I loved what I did. You've got to find what you love. And that is as true for your work as it is for your lovers. Your work is going to fill a large part of your life, and the only way to be truly satisfied is to do what you believe is great work. And the only way to do great work is to love what you do. If you haven't found it yet, keep looking. Don't settle. As with all matters of the heart, you'll know when you find it. And, like any great relationship, it just gets better and better as the years roll on. So keep looking until you find it. Don't settle.

For Steven Spielberg, the famous movie director, it wasn't so obvious. Here is a quote from a speech he made:

The dream is something you never knew was going to come into your life. Dreams always come from behind you, not right between your eyes. It sneaks up on you. But when you have a dream, it doesn't often come at you screaming in your face, "This is who you are, this is what you must be for the rest of your life." Sometimes a dream almost whispers. And I've always said to my kids, the hardest thing to listen to—your instincts, your human personal intuition—always whispers; it never shouts. Very hard to hear. So you have to every day of your lives be ready to hear what whispers in your ear; it very rarely shouts. And if you can listen to the whisper, and if it tickles your heart, and it's something you think you want to do for the rest of your life, then that is going to be what you do for the rest of your life, and we will benefit from everything you do.

HELPING YOU DECIDE WHAT YOU WANT

I once interviewed a person who told me he was very passionate about music but not talented in it. He told me he had taken his grade 8 music exam seven times before he passed. I always remembered it as a story of a person's perseverance for something that he was passionate in. It was also a story that said it is not enough just to have passion; you need to have the innate talent that will help you develop great skill.

I say "innate talent" because there is a huge body of evidence that we are born with certain potential already encoded in our genes. For example, Michael Jordan, the basketball player, was born with a great physique. Of course, he trained very hard as well, but the potential was there. Like him, there are people who are born with very sensitive palates who would make great chefs and sommeliers; people who are strong in visual-spatial imagination who would make great designers and architects; and people who have great mathematical minds, who can see the answers to logical, physics, and engineering problems faster than others. There are people with a great sense of hearing who can distinguish subtle differences in pitch and tone, who would make great musicians, and people who are great with people, who are very good at connecting, interacting, and influencing everyone around them.

I see the innate talent in my own children. My older son has a great visual sense, and he could draw very well from when he was one year old. He loved to draw trucks and cars then, and he had a sense of perspective and proportion even at that young age. My younger son writes very well and has an active imagination. It's amazing if you are a parent and can see very clearly that your children are born with innate talents.

In my life, I've met many people who are doing what it is they love and what it is they are good at, and they are the happiest people I know.

The famous psychologist Abraham Maslow said:

A musician must make music, an artist must paint, a poet must write, if he is to be ultimately at peace with himself. What a man can be, he must be.

18

So if you have not yet discovered what it is you want, think along the lines of what it is you are good at and what it is you enjoy doing.

FLOW

In 2004, Dr. Mihaly Csikszentmihalyi gave a TED Talk where he explained what happens when humans enter a "flow" state. This is an ecstatic state when a person's sense of self disappears, and that person is completely engrossed in an activity he or she is good at.

Dr. Csikszentmihalyi shared several examples, amongst them an Olympic figure skater who said:

> *Everything went right, everything felt good...It's just such a rush, like you feel it could go on and on and on, like you don't want it to stop because it's going so well. It's almost as though you don't have to think, it's like everything goes automatically without thinking...it's like you're on automatic pilot, so you don't have any thoughts. You hear the music but you're not aware that you're hearing it, because it's a part of it all.*

Dr. Csikszentmihalyi and his team interviewed over 8,000 people on the subject and described people who are in a state of flow thus:

- The person is completely immersed in the activity.
- There's an emotional "high."
- There's a great inner clarity on what to do.
- The person has a great sense that he or she has the necessary skills to complete the task well.
- All the concerns melt away.
- There's no sense of time.

You can google "flow" to learn more about it. Scientists who have measured people in a state of flow notice that the brain operates at a different level when someone is in that state.

It is not just the performing artists like the figure skater or the musicians who feel flow. Computer programmers report feeling it quite often, when they are in the "zone," and they can produce prolific amounts of code that work. In fact, some psychologists have shown that about 15 percent of people report feelings of flow *several times a day*, and about 20 percent experience it sometimes. Many people report feeling it at work.

Typically, people who experience flow regularly are doing something they have an innate talent for and have invested a lot of time and energy in, thus becoming highly skilled in it. When you are able to achieve flow constantly, you'll always be in a profound and happy state and you will think life is great. You may already feel lucky every day.

VISIONING THE OUTCOME

What does the end state look like?

You can do this exercise at different stages in your life. Some people suggest you try to imagine what your life is like when you are on your deathbed and work backward from there. I'm almost fifty as I'm writing this, and I tell you that feelings, priorities, and the people and events in our lives change over time, so it is not very useful to imagine too far ahead.

But you can imagine the next five years or ten. What do they look like?

When people say they have a vision for something, what they mean is that they can picture it in their minds. *A vision works best when it is visual,* rather than when it is described with a bunch of words. So when you ask yourself, "How do I *see* myself in five or ten years?" try to imagine pictures in your mind. What does your home look like? What does your family look like? What do your office and your coworkers look like? What do the world and the places you want to go look like? That is the vision you have for yourself and the world you live in.

Now what do you have to do to get there? Create a plan and set it in motion. Put Positive Energy behind it, and good luck will happen!

WHAT ABOUT PRACTICAL CONSIDERATIONS?

There is a stereotype that all Asian parents want their children to be doctors, engineers, or architects. Why is that the case? In my view, it's not that they want the bragging rights of saying that their kids are professionals; it's a more basic desire, which is to ensure that their kids have financial security.

My parents and the people in their generation were born around World War II, and they grew up in hard times. So naturally they wanted us to have better financial security. In their lifetimes, they saw that people who went to college and became professionals, like architects and doctors, did well, so their wish was for us to do the same.

But now that it is my turn as a parent, my experience of the world is very different. My generation has a view that the pace of change is going to get faster and faster, and software and automation are going to make a lot of jobs obsolete. Can we imagine a future of robot doctors and pharmacists? Why not? If you think about it, doctors today are mostly "guessing" with their first diagnosis, based on the observable symptoms, and they have to order blood tests to be sure of what the patients have. Can software and machines advance to such a level that we bypass the doctor completely and the machine takes the blood and comes up with an instant and accurate diagnosis? Can another machine dispense the right drugs immediately thereafter?

That day may not be far off. And if we can imagine that day coming, how can we insist that our children become doctors? When the future is so unclear, how can we insist that our children be anything? For me, I will give my children the same advice that is in this book and trust they will find their own way. In a fast changing world, that may be the most practical advice a parent can give to his children.

INTERNAL AND EXTERNAL CONSIDERATIONS

Whether we are parents thinking about our children's future or we are thinking about our own future, we can look *externally*, think about what the world will be like, and try to make a decision on that basis. Or we can look *internally*, think about what we like and what we are good at, and make a decision from there.

The best situation, of course, is that what we want internally matches with our assessment of what the external environment needs. But when they conflict, how should we choose?

I don't want to pontificate and say that one must always make the choice that is internal. I've met people who are perfectly happy and successful just going along with catering to what the world needs. And I've met people who have chosen less financially successful lives to do what they love. So it's different for different people. You just need to know what the right situation is for you.

"WHAT IF I LIKE TO CLEAN TOILETS?"

One of the favorite topics among parents is what their children want to do. When I say, "I'm OK with anything," I get asked, "What if they want to be a hairdresser or bus driver?" My response is, "If that is what they want to do and they feel happy doing it, why not? They are respectable jobs."

I met a middle-age lady once who told me she used to be a retail assistant, but she found she loved cleaning and became an hourly housekeeper. She says she gets tremendous satisfaction when everything in a house is cleaned properly, particularly the toilets. She told me all her friends think she is crazy for loving to clean toilets, but she says she can't think of doing anything else. Well, her friends may think she is crazy, but her clients love her! They say she's the best housekeeper they've ever had, and they have recommended her to many of their friends. Besides her pay, she also gets all kinds of gifts from her clients, so she thinks of herself as very lucky. If you're doing something you love and you are highly appreciated for it, wouldn't you think of yourself as lucky?

So I don't believe we can generalize and say that one job is good and another is not, even for our own children. If people discover joy in whatever they do and they are good at it, that is the best situation of all.

Also, we shouldn't be judgmental about what other people do. If they chose it willingly and find satisfaction in doing it, it's a great thing. We should envy them.

SCIENCE

In this chapter, I've drawn from identity psychology.

CONCLUSION

The world defines you by what you do. It's again partly to do with the evolution of the human race. People want to know what you do so they know how you are contributing to making things better. *They want to know whether they can benefit from you.* That's why it is the first question people ask when they meet you. It's also how you are introduced in formal settings and how the media reports news about you. It's your name, followed by your profession.

Once you're able to find the thing you want to commit your life to, you will have a greater sense of your identity and you will feel more confident about your life. You can relate to all the things you encounter in a more contextual, relevant, and meaningful way. You will then be able to recognize the lucky breaks when they come.

A great salesperson who loves to do sales and who has honed his sales skills in a small company might get a lucky break when his talent and passion are spotted by a boss from a larger company and given a much larger portfolio of clients. A musician who is constantly in a state of flow and producing amazing music might get a lucky break from a producer who wants to promote his music. An accountant who is great with numbers and has a great understanding of how business works might be asked to join a fast-growing start-up with complex accounting needs and given shares in the company. An entrepreneur who loves inventions and has become really great at developing them might get a lucky break from an investor who is willing to back his ideas.

When you know the luck you need, your mind is focused on it, and you'll instinctively find yourself in situations where those lucky breaks might occur. People who are interested in what you do will also find their way to you. Accordingly, then, the odds of lucky breaks become high.

**Know the luck you want so that you will
benefit from it when it comes.**

WHERE DOES LUCK COME FROM: PART I-IDEAS

*Wit is the sudden marriage of ideas which, before their
union, were not perceived to have any relation.*

—MARK TWAIN

YOU KNOW WHAT you want to do, and you are starting to put Positive
Energy behind it. Now you need to have a series of achievements that
will bring you to your big lucky break.

The achievements will come from constant innovations and improvements in what you do. You need to demonstrate continually *new
ideas* that work.

Ideas drive the allocation of resources, so if you can come up with
ideas that will lead to innovation and improvements, you will be entrust-
ed with many resources. With these resources, you must demonstrate
you can execute your ideas well. When you do, you are on your way to
getting your big lucky break.

But where do you get new ideas all the time?

COLLECTING DOTS

This is the most often quoted segment of the commencement speech
Steve Jobs gave in 2005 that I referred to in the previous chapter:

You can't connect the dots looking forward; you can only connect them looking backward. So you have to trust that the dots will somehow connect in your future.

He goes on to tell the story of how he "dropped in" on a calligraphy class in college because he was interested in it. He said he had no idea how calligraphy would have any practical application in his life, but ten years later, when he was designing the Macintosh computer, it came back to him, and he incorporated it.

"It was the first computer with beautiful typography," he said. And he sold a lot of it.

Taking that thinking further, I arrive at the idea that this works only if you have a lot of dots to connect with in the first place. If you haven't experienced much in life, if you haven't read a lot of books, if you haven't dropped in on many classes, you won't have many dots to connect with. And if you don't have many dots to connect with, your ability to constantly come up with new ideas is diminished.

So, to become great at connecting dots, you first need to *collect* dots. In a later part of the same speech, Steve Jobs said:

Much of what I stumbled into by following my curiosity and intuition turned out to be priceless later on.

He used the word "stumbled" to convey that there wasn't a lot of planning. He simply let his curiosity and interest guide him. So in collecting dots, you cannot always be motivated by practical considerations. This is because you don't always know what can come in useful in the future. What might seem whimsical at one time could really be the important dot you need to connect with to achieve a breakthrough idea in the future. In fact, you can think of it this way: Everyone else would have gone for all the logical and practical courses and would know how to connect with those ideas. *It remains that you need to know about impractical, unrelated, and whimsical ideas to come out with unexpected results.*

Since there is no way you can be certain what might come in useful in the future, the best course is to follow your "curiosity and intuition" and participate in anything that interests you. If you like the activity, you will participate in it with intensity, and you will remember what you learn very well.

LUCK IS WIDE

Steve Jobs also said:

> *You have to trust in something—your gut, destiny, life, karma, whatever. This approach has never let me down, and it has made all the difference in my life.*

Whatever it is you want to do, don't second-guess it too much. If you like it, it will be good, and it will be a useful dot in one way or another down the road. *This is because everything is connected.* The more you know *across* different spheres, the more you will have a holistic view of life, and the more you will be able to see the interconnectedness.

I spoke to a mathematician who learned music when he was young, and he saw that music was mathematical. He felt that it made him a better mathematician as well as a better musician. In my own experience, I've enjoyed writing and telling stories since I was young. When I started work, I found that this skill helped me greatly in my sales presentations. When I entered the finance industry, it gave me an edge because everyone else was great with numbers and charts but not so with words.

When you are young especially, do not get stuck in a narrow position. Find ways to experience new things and meet new people. Collect as many dots as you can in terms of knowledge, experiences, and contacts.

They will form your reservoir for future ideas.

LUCK IS DEEP

If you know a little of everything, the luck you will get is likely to be shallow. To score very big, you need to have deep insights into a particular domain. The biggest inventors, innovators, and creative people in the world did not suddenly have world-changing ideas out of nowhere.

For example, when the people at IBM went to Bill Gates to ask him to develop the operating system (OS) for their personal computer in 1980, Bill Gates had already been developing software for five years and was quite well known in the industry. He understood what an OS was and what it did. So it wasn't like Bill Gates woke up one morning and suddenly thought, "I think I'll develop an OS for IBM."

Also, Albert Einstein did not just arrive at the theory of relativity out of nowhere. He had been working on it for a very long time, and he was already the world's foremost physicist. When he sought the answers to the complex questions surrounding relativity, he already had many pieces of the puzzle in his head. And then the aha moment hit, and he connected all the relevant pieces and came out with something big. That's how it is with many great ideas. The people who were able to exploit them were often experts in their field or a related field, and they "connected a dot" with something else and created something new.

If you are not a deep expert in a particular area, few people will invest big amounts with you, so you will not get access to the deep pockets you need to fund your ideas.

WHERE DO *BIG* IDEAS COME FROM?

Big ideas are both deep and wide.

First, as I've said, it comes from having acquired very deep knowledge and expertise in a particular domain. Second, it comes from dots, and there are two ways you can succeed with them: you can *discover* them, or you can *connect* them. Those who discover dots are at the cutting edge of their fields. For example, Michael Faraday discovered in the mid-1800s that when a wire carrying an electric current is placed next to a single magnetic pole, the wire will rotate. This was a new dot. People did not know this prior to his discovery.

But once the dot was discovered and other people were able to learn about it, it was about connecting that dot with other dots to create something new. In the case of Michael Faraday's discovery, later inventors took his discovery and invented the electric motor and eventually the huge electric generators that produce electricity for everyone.

Steve Jobs, in an interview with *Wired* magazine in 1996 said:

Creativity is just connecting things. When you ask creative people how they did something, they feel a little guilty because they didn't really do it, they just saw something. It seemed obvious to them after a while. That's because they were able to connect experiences they've had and synthesize new things.

So that's where the big ideas come from. You can be at the forefront of science, medicine, archaeology, materials, and all the other fields of knowledge and make discoveries (dots) for the human race to connect, or you have to be especially good at connecting the dots that are already there. Either way, you need to have invested a lot of effort and time and become an expert in the domain of your choice.

BIG IDEAS COME FROM SMALL INNOVATIONS

Another favorite quote from Steve Jobs that people like to use is the line he said to John Sculley, who was working at Pepsi at the time, to try to convince him to join Apple. He said, "Do you want to sell sugar water for the rest of your life, or do you want to come with me and change the world?"

In my experience, though, people who think like that right from the beginning won't do very well. When Steve Jobs said that line to John Sculley, Apple was already a listed company and quite sizable. It makes sense that he had thoughts of changing the world. But that's not the case for a new business or project.

Most people will just feel that their product or service idea has merit and has a place in the market. This was true of Apple when it first launched. Steve Jobs tried to raise money for his idea and had tremendous difficulty doing it. There was no changing the world. He and Steve Wozniak, his cofounder, needed to sell a few computers to show there was a basic demand and that it made sense for investors to invest in them.

It was the same with the Google founders Larry Page and Sergey Brin. When they first came out with their product, they were not very confident about the business themselves. We know this because one year after the founding of Google, they wanted to sell it for US$1 million. The deal did not go through, which was lucky for them because today the company is worth over US$500 billion.

One of my favorite examples of small innovations that led to world-changing results is how the Mongols created the largest empire on Earth in the 1200s. Their conquered lands stretched from Asia all the way to Europe. In the battles they fought, they didn't always outnumber their enemies. In fact, there were many battles where they were the smaller force. But they were able to strike with ferocity and move with tremendous speed.

What was their key innovation that allowed them to do that? Up until that time, wars were limited by the distance that horses could ride in a day, which was about 30 km. Human infantry soldiers could also move only so far. So armies had to set up camp for the day and move again the next. This was terribly slow, and the enemies would be alerted early and have plenty of time to plan their defense. To extend their range and speed, the Mongols used mainly cavalry (soldiers on horseback), and each soldier brought five extra horses with him. That way they could travel for over 150 km a day. With this, they struck with great speed and could advance on a city before it had the chance to prepare a proper defense.

That was the innovation! *Bring extra horses!* With that, they tried it on a few cities and found they could conquer them easily. The early success gave them the confidence to go farther, and eventually they went so far that they created the largest empire ever up to that point in history.

So you should not fret and think, "How am I going to think up a world-changing idea?" The world-changing ideas don't start that way. They are usually formed from simple insights into how people would use a particular product or service differently. Just focus on making little innovations and improvements to what you are doing now, and try to connect a new dot now and then. Eventually they will all add up to something significant.

HOW CAN YOU THINK MORE CREATIVELY?

If luck comes from new ideas, what can you do to be more creative? The wrong answer would be *to work harder*. In fact, working harder is counterproductive to creative thinking. Your mind would be too focused on the job at hand, and you wouldn't have the bandwidth to think about something new.

A lot of research is emerging now that you actually need to do what a *lazy* person does. You need to sleep a lot, daydream, go on vacations, have fun, spend time with friends and family, exercise, listen to music, and simply just play and have fun. The difference from a lazy person is that you would be considering a problem while you were doing all that.

To me, that's the best advice for work-life balance I can find! You upload the details of the problem you are working on into your head and go back and do all the fun and restful things listed above! The creative solution may come to you when you are doing those things. You may get that aha moment in the shower, that special insight when you are doodling or walking, that "OMG, it is so obvious!" insight from talking to a family member.

Scientists tell us that when we are doing the "lazy" or "mindless" things, we are tapping into the creative part of our brains. And if the problem we need to solve is in the background of our minds at the same time, it gets infused with the creative-thinking process, and we see the solution.

For me, I don't do any of the important thinking at my desk. I hold a particular thought or problem I am working on in my head, and I go about my day. There are many pockets of waiting time when I am not doing anything, like waiting for the train, waiting for a meeting to start, waiting for a friend to show up, or waiting for my coffee to be served. There's also a lot of free mental time when I am doing personal stuff like exercising, helping with the household chores, and just being on the toilet. I do the mental processing at these times, and I find that I can sort through a lot of stuff in my head.

If I need a shot of inspiration, there are three things I do. One is listening to rock music, another is reading, and the last is sleeping. Sleeping is particularly useful. When I wake up in the morning after a good night's rest, I immediately think about the problem I am working on, and I often get a burst of insight that will help me see the solutions I need.

SCIENCE

I've continued with my theme from the first two chapters. It's about human evolution. People want to know how you are making things better. If you can show them, you will attract resources from them.

Your ability to make things better comes from creativity, and creativity comes from connecting or discovering dots. You collect dots by experiencing life, learning things that interest you, and developing deep competencies in a particular domain. And you connect dots by constantly adding new elements to what you do. At some point, when you have connected enough dots, you will get your lucky break.

Luck comes from creative ideas.

WHERE DOES LUCK COME FROM: PART II-PEOPLE

I've found that luck is quite predictable. If you want more luck, take more chances. Be more active. Show up more often.

—BRIAN TRACY

IN THE PREVIOUS chapter, I said you'll find luck in ideas. The better the ideas you have, the more you are able to attract talent and resources.

Another source of luck is people. The more people you know and who know you, the greater your ability to discover opportunities.

WHAT KIND OF PEOPLE?
All kinds of people!

In the first chapter, I already talked about hanging with people who are full of Positive Energy. And in the previous chapter, we talked about collecting dots in terms of the skills and knowledge that interest you. You can see *people as part of the dots* you have to collect. You may not know how a person may become relevant and "lucky" for you in the future, but you just have to trust that they will.

And as with the dots of knowledge and skills, you should connect with anyone who interests you. Don't be a snob and just connect with those who have power and money. They may not be of any use at all. Instead, open your mind to meeting all kinds of people from all kinds of backgrounds, and be intensely curious about what they do and how they think. Do not keep to your small circle of friends or think that people outside your industry can have no contributions to your career and life. Seek out and connect with people who are full of Positive Energy. You will be surprised by what you can learn and the opportunities you can get.

TURN UP AND ENGAGE DEEPLY

Is there a school reunion coming up? Be sure to attend it! It's one of the greatest places to meet people because there is already a high level of trust that people from the same school have for one another.

If you haven't done so well in life, you might not feel like going for fear of others looking down on you, but that's really in your own head. Think about it this way: you could be the most successful person in the room, and there'd still be people who want to point to your weaknesses and put you down. So it's really quite a futile thing to try to manage what other people think. If you've done well and you want to go to a reunion to show off, you won't have much luck either. People may say nice things to you, but if they sense that you are there to brag, they will avoid you. So stop thinking about you, and just go and engage with your old friends! You'll find interesting stories, important lessons, and great contacts.

In general, turn up at social, industry, or networking events as much as you can. It's a numbers game. The more people you meet, the greater the odds of good things happening.

Now, when you go to these events, my experience is that it is better to engage deeply with only one or two people than to try to meet a big number of them. It's useless to meet a lot of people if afterward they have no memory of you. It is better to get to know someone well. The numbers work out better that way.

Each of us has about 35 people in our lives whom we know well enough to recommend high-value contacts to, and we have about 350 Facebook friends we don't mind making general introductions to. So the trick is to know a person well enough to tap into these numbers. If you get to know two people well enough at an event, you will have access to 700 reasonable contacts. If you just have a cursory meeting with someone, you will not be able to tap into these numbers. That person will not feel comfortable making any kind of introductions if he doesn't have a good sense of you.

So keep the 35/350 number in mind, and find people to engage deeply with. Be very interested in the stories they have to share, and be very enthusiastic in sharing your stories and ideas if they are interested to know. If you can spend enough time with two people at every event you go to, you will find that your contacts for anything you need go up quite significantly.

PERSONAL STORIES

I went to a high school reunion a few years ago, and I thoroughly enjoyed it. I haven't seen my ex-schoolmates for over twenty-five years, and many of them have become very prominent people in their chosen fields. I was placed next to a doctor who was a cancer specialist at the dinner table. The organizers had arranged us randomly, so it was pure chance that I sat next to him. We spent most of the reunion talking to each other, with me finding out about the world of cancer and he about the world of finance and start-ups that I come from. From talking to him, I realized that of the many friends and contacts I had, I didn't have one who was a doctor, so what a doctor does, especially a cancer specialist, fascinated me.

I would have been happy just to have met a doctor and learned more about cancer at the dinner, but this doctor friend called me a few weeks later and asked me if I was keen to join the board of a prominent cancer charity of which he was chairman. I said yes, and from there a whole new world opened up for me.

I got to know about cancer and various other diseases. I got introductions to a few excellent doctors for when my family and I needed them. I was introduced to the boards of other charities and expanded my network further. And I am currently exploring business opportunities in medical technology. Best of all, I met fascinating people from other fields that I normally would not meet. These were passionate doctors, social workers, and researchers who cared deeply about their work and their patients and who are working very hard to make treatments better. In return, I am glad to be able to make my own contributions, in my own way, to the field.

Another time I met up with an old army mate (Singaporean males have to serve two years in the army as national service), and he told me about a business idea he had. I connected him to a young entrepreneur I had met through another event, and the entrepreneur decided to take the idea on and start a company. The business is now growing very well, and I am a significant shareholder.

I can go on, but you get the picture. Some of the biggest opportunities in my life have happened simply because I turned up at events and engaged deeply with someone.

BE THE GUY WHOM OTHERS WANT TO CONNECT WITH

So you know to seek out people with great Positive Energy and connect with them. But once you find them, will they want to connect with *you?* What is your *reputation?* You have to think about that because it precedes you. The people you meet may have heard about you from others and formed an impression of you beforehand. Would that impression help or hinder you?

People will want to connect with you if you have a good reputation for getting things done, for being good with people, and for being generous and happy to share the fruits. If your reputation is that you are distrustful of people, full of angst about the world, and selfish with rewards, people will avoid you.

Some people tell me, "I don't have much of a reputation to speak of." But you do! You may not have a public reputation where strangers know about you, but you have a personal reputation with your friends and family, teachers, colleagues, and business associates. What do they think of you?

The following is a good test for your personal reputation. Imagine if you had an idea for a business or project and you went to your friends and family for money, would they invest in you? I've had interesting experiences with young entrepreneurs on this. Sometimes after hearing a pitch for money, I would ask, "Are your parents or relatives investing in this business?" Often, the answer I get is, "Oh, I don't want to bother them with this," or "Oh, I don't think they will understand this," or "I don't think they will be interested." It's funny because here I have the young entrepreneur telling me he is going to make millions with his idea, yet he says he doesn't want to "bother" his family to get some of those millions for themselves! To me, this means that either this young entrepreneur is not very confident about his idea, or he doesn't have a great personal reputation in his family.

On the other hand, I've also met young entrepreneurs who were able to raise good money from their families and friends. They often say their friends and families don't really understand the business ideas they have and hence didn't invest because of the ideas. They invested because they know and trust the entrepreneurs. It doesn't mean the entrepreneurs will succeed for sure; it just means that their friends and family trust them enough to risk some money with them.

Do not think that raising money from family and friends is easy. Just think about your own family and friends. How many of them will *you* invest money with? You will realize the number is quite small. So think about your personal reputation. Do you have a reputation for great ideas and good Positive Energy to get things done? Are you the kind of person to whom people say, "Hey, if you ever have a project, please remember to include me"? Strive to be that person so that others will seek you out, connect with you, and share resources with you.

HIRING AND FUNDING

When I started work in the early '90s, the way you got a job was through sending out resumes to companies that were hiring. But emerging research shows that interviewing complete strangers is not a very good way of hiring. It is just not possible to know enough about the person in the short time an interview takes to make such an important decision.

So I see more and more companies hiring based on the personal networks of their staff. I can't find any official numbers to support this, but I definitely see it as a trend. When the companies need to hire new people, they broadcast it to the staff and ask if they have friends to recommend. And if good staff will recommend their friends, it means two things: the staff is confident enough about the friend to stake his personal reputation within the company on it, and the staff likes the company enough to want to recommend it to his friend.

It may seem like luck, but if you are a young person, you should know that many of the job opportunities that are going to come your way in life will likely come through friends and contacts rather than job listings.

It is the same with business and project funding. During the Internet and app booms, a lot of "beauty parades" were held where young people went in front of venture capitalists (VCs) to present their ideas. But very few people actually got funded that way. Rather, most of the businesses that got funded came from these three categories:

- Entrepreneurs who were friends and long-term contacts of the VCs. Many of them were alumni.
- The bootstrapped founder who had launched his business and achieved momentum. This was easy for the VCs to put money in since there was already market acceptance.
- Serial entrepreneurs who had a strong track record of success.

So it's seldom the idea *alone* that gets funded. It's the entrepreneur who knows the VCs, and whom the VCs know. Some people say it is unfair, that mediocre founders known to the VCs get funded but great ideas from other people don't. People who say this are usually the entrepreneurs who didn't get funded. And they think that their idea is great because they are very close to it, but it may not be.

Here is a simple example to illustrate why it is more important to fund the person rather than the idea. Take coffee as an idea. People like coffee, so there's clearly a demand for it. So someone may have the idea to open a café to sell coffee and cakes. That's the idea, and lots of people have the same idea and have tried it. But why is it that some people go bankrupt with just one store and others create massive chains like Starbucks? You'll find that the answer to this question is that success is not just about the idea. It is about the person who is executing the idea, whether he has what it takes to succeed.

So you may really be the right person with the right idea. *But if the people with money don't know you, you are really asking them to fund you based on your idea alone.* This seldom works. You have to invest time in getting to know the people with influence and money so that they know you and trust you, and then your odds of getting funded will go up.

BURNISH YOUR PERSONAL REPUTATION

If you are working on a huge project or you are running a business that's very popular, you will be featured in the media a lot, and you will come to have a public reputation. But most people don't get to those kinds of levels. The projects you manage are likely to be smaller, and if there's interest from the media, it is likely to be sporadic. This is still great for the project and the business, so you should certainly take these media opportunities when they come and make the best of them.

With infrequent media exposure, you won't be able to cultivate a public reputation. A stranger who reads the news about you may take note of the project or the business but not of you. This is like the scores of people who get featured in the press on a daily basis. We don't really remember who they are because we don't know them.

But it's different when we *do* know them. We will be reminded of them and our relationship with them and think they must be doing very well with the media exposure. This is how you can burnish your reputation with the people who know you. You may not be able to meet up with them frequently, but if they read about you, they will be reminded of you. Your 350 Facebook friends may share the news and talk about their relationship with you.

There is a kind of halo effect from being in the news. It's partly the exposure, and it's partly the way journalists write the stories. They want to write in a way that causes others to read, so they will try to give stories interesting angles.

When I was an employee working for others, there were several occasions where I was featured in magazines or newspapers (this was before the Internet). There were a few unique marketing executions I was responsible for that got reported, and there were also a few personal features written by journalists who wanted to write about people with interesting jobs or hobbies. I believe the media exposure helped me in being more visible to my bosses and gave me opportunities that others did not get.

When I ran my own businesses, the media exposure became even more important. Not only did it increase sales, it also brought many lucky offers of help and investments.

So my experience has been that being featured in the media is highly useful. You shouldn't shun the media. In fact, you should try to cultivate it by constantly pitching your stories to the media. You should not be afraid to send out press releases. Journalists love to receive them because they get story ideas. They may not cover the story exactly as you hoped for, but they may find another angle that's equally interesting. It's a great way to keep you in the minds of all your contacts and promote your project or business as well.

RICH HABITS

I quoted from Thomas C. Corley in an earlier chapter. He did a five year interview with 233 millionaires and authored the book *Change Your*

Habits, Change Your Life. In an article for the BusinessInsider website on 13 February 2016, he says

> *Luck hides inside new relationships. Meeting the right person at the right time, requires that you … meet people. People do not just drop in your lap and, voilà, luck happens. You have to go out and find them. You find them by joining networking groups, by volunteering at non-profits, by taking seminars, at fund-raisers, when you take up tennis, or golf. You find the right person at the right time by doing new and novel things.*

SCIENCE

Again, I've drawn largely from the idea that humans want to evolve. We want things to be better for ourselves personally and for all human kind in general. So we think of everything around us in those terms. The question at the backs of our minds when we meet someone is, "Is this the kind of person who would make things better for me?" If you meet someone who is, you'll want to connect with him or her. Similarly, if you are that kind of person, others will want to connect with you.

Once you understand that, it's basically mathematics: learn *more* things and meet *more* people. Start initiating projects and putting Positive Energy behind them. Good luck will flow to you from many different directions!

Luck comes from people who know you and trust you.

THE SECOND MOST IMPORTANT
THING ABOUT LUCK: BELIEF

*You've got to ask yourself one question. Do
I feel lucky? Well, do ya, punk?*

—DIRTY HARRY

YES, I DO! Feel lucky, that is.

In fact, I think of myself as one of the luckiest person alive. I can point to so many things that have happened to me that are tremendously lucky.

Have there been unlucky things that have happened to me? Yes, of course, but I see those things as good as well, because they were necessary for my education in life, and to build my resilience and wisdom.

If Positive Energy is the most important thing about luck, this is the second. You have to see yourself as a lucky person. You can't project Positive Energy consistently and sustainably if you feel that you are fundamentally an unlucky person and underserving of great luck.

SELF-PERCEPTION

If you see yourself as a lucky person, you will see opportunities everywhere. Even in negative events, you will see the silver lining and consider yourself lucky that it is not all bad.

If you believe you are not a lucky person, you will see challenges everywhere. Even in positive events, you will see the difficulties and consider yourself unlucky that you have encountered the event.

It's like my story about the Positive and Negative Energy young men who found the potatoes in the first chapter. They both found the same two scrawny potatoes, so it wasn't about the potatoes. The young man with Positive Energy saw it as lucky, developed the next course of action, and cooked a big pot of soup for everyone. The young man with Negative Energy saw it as unlucky and kicked the potatoes aside. Worse, he cursed his luck, which reinforced the negativity he had about his life.

Do you see yourself as a lucky person? This is an important question, so you might want to take a while to think about it. It goes to the question of belief. It is the belief you have about your own life.

BELIEF

Psychologists and sociologists have studied human belief and found it to be a very powerful force. When we believe something, we will hold on to it despite great hardship and defend it with great effort. Even when we are presented with evidence to the contrary, we will not let go of our beliefs easily. New beliefs can fundamentally change our personality, worldview, and the very direction we take in our lives.

Once we have a belief, we will look for confirmation the belief is true. So if we believe gods are responsible for everything in our lives, we will see the work of gods everywhere. If we believe our government is evil, we will see evil in everything they do. If we think a friend is untrustworthy, we will interpret all his actions to match this viewpoint.

When we are shown evidence that contradicts our beliefs, such as when the government actually does something good for the people, we will not accept that our belief is wrong. Instead, we will explain it in a way that fits our beliefs. For example, we may say they are doing it only because the election is around the corner, or we may subscribe to a conspiracy theory that says the good deed secretly benefits a particular family member of a key politician.

Religion and politics are two of the most powerful beliefs people have. And we can see that these beliefs are entrenched in people who believe in them. Here are some lesser known, and perhaps more interesting, effects of beliefs.

Placebo. When doctors test a new drug, they will have three groups of test subjects. One group will receive the new drug, one will receive nothing, and the third will receive a placebo. The placebo is an inactive drug that is given to test subjects to see if the simple act of believing they are receiving treatment will achieve positive results. If the new drug is to be proven to work, it has to show it has greater efficacy than the placebo.

The placebo test group will usually report better results than the group that received no treatment at all. Often, test subjects who believe they have received treatment will get better simply as a result of that belief.

School results. Many studies have shown that if the teachers expect their students to do better, they will. It's called the Pygmalion effect. Also, if something were to cause the students themselves to believe they can do better, they will too.

Sports. Athletes who have been given placebos end up performing better. Motivational words that cause the athletes to believe in their ability to outperform their usual standards can also result in improvements.

Inter-personal attraction. If you think that you are attractive to the opposite sex, you will succeed in attracting the opposite sex!

WHY DO BELIEFS WORK?

Beliefs work because they become self-fulfilling prophecies. A self-fulfilling prophecy is a belief that comes true because we are acting as if it is already true. *Our expectation that we will see a particular outcome changes our behavior.* This will shape the way we interact with others and the way they see us. Along the way, the people around us, knowing our beliefs, give us filtered feedback which reinforces our beliefs. Over time, a set of events will happen that will conclude with the belief becoming true.

What makes self-fulfilling prophecies work? There are several reasons.

Numbers. A man who believes he is physically attractive to the opposite sex acts in a confident way. He is not afraid to approach women and speak to them. As he speaks to many women, some will come to like him for various reasons. This may lead him to conclude that he is, in fact, physically attractive to women; but the real reason for his success may simply be the number of attempts he makes to meet women.

Confidence. When we believe in something, we will act in a confident way. This confidence can powerfully influence the people around us. This is especially so if the thing we are confident about is something unclear or untested. For example, when a startup founder is very confident about an idea, he can mobilize tremendous resources to himself. The people who join him may or may not believe in the project in the same way that the founder does, but they are persuaded by the founder's confidence. (Confidence, of course, is a form of Positive Energy).

Focus. At the personal level, when we believe in something greatly, we will focus all our energies on it. That's how I think placebos work (scientists are still studying the placebo effect and haven't been able to definitively explain it). Those who have been cured by placebos have not been given any treatment at all. So somehow they must have mobilized the resources they had in their bodies to fight the illnesses.

A page in WebMD explains it this way:

One of the most common theories is that the placebo effect is due to a person's expectations. If a person expects a pill to do something, then it's possible that the body's own chemistry can cause effects similar to what a medication might have caused.

It is the same when a person of authority tells a class of students that they can perform better at school. The students focus better and do better as a result.

Affirmation. When we have a belief, we are often able to find others who share in the same beliefs. The affirmation that comes from them gives us assurance that we are doing the right thing. It gives us motivation and energy to carry on.

IT'S A KIND OF MENTAL TRAINING

Let's get back to you! Do you expect lucky things to happen to you? Do you expect that you will always achieve everything that you set out to do? Based on the above rationale, it is important that you do. If you expect luck, you will behave in a way that will help you get luck. If you don't expect it, you will behave in a way that won't help you get it.

What if you don't think you are lucky?

Let's try and explain why you have this belief. It is likely that you have encountered a few events in your life that you have interpreted as unlucky. You may then have generalized those experiences to your entire life and decided in your mind, "I will never have any good luck, so it is safer that I do not try."

This mental heuristic that you formed in your mind is a coping mechanism. You reject anything new immediately in order to conserve your resources. Since you believe you won't have any luck, there is no point expending time, effort or money grappling with new things. You will look for evidence that your decision to do nothing is right. For example, you might point to many people who have failed in various things as justification for not trying new things. You will also gather with people with the same belief as you, so that you have social affirmation in your belief.

When you make up your mind that lucky things do not happen to you, you will stop spotting opportunities. You will start on the opposite of a self-fulfilling prophecy, which is a self-defeating prophecy. You will embark on a course of action that will lead to bad luck. You may not even be conscious of it, but little decisions you make will train your mind to ignore new possibilities and opportunities. The first few times you do it, it might be conscious, and you think "no, I won't do that". After a few times, your mind will filter out anything new for you automatically.

Your mind then becomes trained on your daily routine. On the bright side, this can conserve considerable resources for you in the short term as you do not spend or risk any resources on anything new or different from what you are doing. But in a fast changing world, nothing stays the same for long, so you might find that the security and familiarity you cling to is threaten by new things soon enough. You don't go out looking for them, but they find you. When they do, you will think of these things as bad luck, because you did not want them and you are not prepared for them.

In a rapidly changing world, the mantra is "adapt or die". You have to open your hearts and minds to new possibilities all the time. You have to develop an optimistic belief that no matter what comes, you will be able to handle it and it will be good. When you have that belief, then life becomes exciting! There will be successes and there will be lessons learnt. But you must believe that it will always work out one way or another. Then, you will see luck, and luck will find you.

EXERCISES TO HELP YOU THINK LUCKY

There are many suggestions in this book. Open your mind to them and try them.

Here is another suggestion. List the things in your life you do consider lucky. This will train your mind to look for the good and lucky things in your life, rather than just focus on your challenges. It makes you aware that good and lucky things are in fact happening to you.

If you really cannot think of anything positive, it might be because your mind is so hardwired to looking at negative things. Try this instead: think of how much *worse* your current situation could be! For example, if you've had an accident recently and broken an arm, try to think of it as lucky that you didn't break more parts of your body, or die. Try to list as many items as you can.

As you do this, you are training your mind to see things positively and see positive things. Thereafter, the first few times new things come into your life, you might need to make a conscious effort to assess them and think "Hey, I think this could be good for me." As you continue to train your mind this way, it will start to spot opportunities, and in time, you will do it instinctively.

THINGS TO BELIEVE IN

There are two kinds of things that keep entrepreneurs up at night. One is worry about the various challenges that their businesses have, and the other is excitement about a new idea. Most entrepreneurs, artists, scientists, leaders and many people in the creative fields would have experienced times when they have been gripped by an idea so much that they stay awake the whole night. It is an idea that possesses them, and they are compelled to think about it, talk to people about it, and make it happen.

So that's one thing to believe in. An idea that grips you that your entire being believes has to happen.

Sometimes you meet a person who has that idea and you are persuaded by that person to join him in his quest to make the idea happen.

Whether you believe in an idea or person, the basis of your success will be that you believe in yourself, that you are worthy of success and good luck, and that you have the ability to contribute and make good things happen.

When you have these beliefs, you will let great experiences and luck enter into your life.

SCIENCE

I have drawn largely from cognitive psychology, in particular the study of belief, self-perception and self-fulfilling prophecies.

48

CONCLUSION

If you are educated enough to read this book and you have money to buy it, it is likely that you are like most people: you have some good luck and some bad. So if you think of yourself as "mostly unlucky", it's probably a matter of perception and belief. You can change this belief right now by making a decision to think of yourself as lucky. When you do so, you will train your mind to look out for lucky things. When you become good at that, you will notice the big breaks when they come.

This is the last chapter of the section I call Luck Basics.

You have great Positive Energy, you know what you want, you have great ideas and you have great contacts. Now, believe in yourself, believe in your ideas, believe in your team, and believe that good luck will happen to you.

Great luck will start rolling in soon!

Believe that you are lucky, and you will be.

PART II

CIRCUMSTANTIAL LUCK

THE LUCK YOU WERE BORN WITH

To hell with circumstances; I create opportunities.

—Bruce Lee

US PRESIDENT DONALD Trump is a lucky man.

Although he attributes a lot of his success to his skills, like a lot of businessmen do, the fact is that he was born with many lucky advantages.

He was born rich. He said that his father gave him US$1 million to start his own business, but others say the number is closer to US$100 million. Whatever the number is, it is clear that Donald Trump was born rich and had the privileges of an upper-class upbringing.

He was born in America. If he had been born in Kenya or Syria, his chances of success would have been much slimmer.

He is male. He was born in the 1940s, and when he was growing up in the '50s and '60s, there were significant advantages that men had over women.

He is part of the majority race. In America, this means he is white. There are always systemic advantages a member of the majority race has over those in the minority races in any country. In America, this was very pronounced in the years when Donald Trump was growing up.

He is tall, at 1.91 meters. Studies show that tall people make more money and are generally more successful than shorter people.

He started his real estate business in the '70s. The United States had a population of about 200 million people at the beginning of the '70s and has about 330 million people today. This huge increase in population is a boon for businessmen in the real estate business.

BIRTH LUCK

If there are a couple of things we can think of as pure luck that we have absolutely nothing to do with, it's the genes we inherited from our ancestors and the circumstances in which we were born. Other than those listed in Donald Trump's example above, here are some other things you could be born with that make you lucky or unlucky.

Your looks. If you were born good-looking, it is a well-researched fact that you will have greater luck in attracting the opposite sex and in work opportunities.

Your health. If you were born with no genetic defects and you don't suffer from any long-term major or minor illnesses, you can consider yourself very lucky. Many people have to grapple with some kind of physical issues. The big ones are easy to recognize, but there are also small ailments like short-sightedness, acne, asthma, sweaty palms, eczema, irritable bowels, or allergies that can be energy-sapping to manage. Consider yourself lucky if you have none of the big issues. Consider yourself truly blessed when you don't even have the small ones.

Your IQ. Studies show that this is mostly genetic. You can affect a few points with diet, exercise, and other factors in your environment, but there is no way you can fundamentally change your IQ. Just to be clear, the links between IQ and gender or race have been debunked. You can find high IQ people in both genders and in all races.

Your birth order. It has been shown that a person's birth order within a family can have important effects on his or her personality. For example, the firstborn is likely to be more independent and driven to succeed.

Your innate abilities. As described in chapter 2, people have innate abilities they are born with. Some people have a good musical sense, while others have great visual capabilities; some are born with excellent physiques, and others have sensitive palates and more.

Your life growing up. Did you have the opportunities to be educated? Did you feel safe living in your neighborhood? Was your family able to afford the basic necessities and a bit more? Did you have proper health care whenever you needed it? Did you have a loving and supportive family? If you answered mostly yes, consider yourself lucky.

All the above factors are not of our own doing. We were all born with a set of genes and circumstances that gave us advantages or disadvantages in life.

THE TOP 1 PERCENT OF HUMANITY

I used to go to India quite often in the mid-2000s for business. I've traveled all over India, but I mostly went to Mumbai. Mumbai had about sixteen million people in the mid-2000s. But half of them—that's eight million—lived in the slums or on the streets. My colleagues told me a person can live in the slums for around twenty-five US dollars a month, which is less than one dollar a day. You can get a full meal with rice and curried dishes for only fifteen cents in the slums, so that adds up to forty-five cents for three meals a day. The rest goes towards other necessities like clothes and rental. (All numbers here are based on my experience of Mumbai in the mid-2000s. The numbers may have changed.)

In those days, there were very few decent mid-priced hotels in Mumbai for visitors to stay in. Consequently, we had to stay at the top hotels, which charged about US$350 a night. I worked out that for my one night's stay in the hotel, someone in the slums could survive for over a year.

Recently, I was on a visit to China, and a tour guide showed me a book that contained a picture of men hauling a boat along the shallow part of the river Yangtze. The men were wearing nothing but loincloths. The tour guide asked, "Why do you think the men are almost naked?"

The replies my group gave were, "It is tradition," "It is too hot in the summer," and "They had a better grip on the ropes." The correct answer was that they were too poor to afford work clothes. My group had visitors from Singapore, France, Australia, the United States, and New Zealand—all first-world countries with rich residents. Nobody guessed that the answer was because the people were too poor to afford clothes.

According to the people from the Global Rich List, if you make an annual income of US$32,400, you belong to the top 1 percent of income earners in the world. That's just US$2,700 a month if you divide the annual income by twelve. If you are educated enough to read this book, chances are that you belong to this group or are very close to it.

You may not feel rich when you compare yourself with the people around you. But if you compare yourself with the rest of the world, you should know that at this moment of your existence, you are better off than 99 percent of the people who live on this earth. There are a lot of very poor people in the world who are still struggling with very basic needs like food, clean water, and sanitation. Sometimes all you need to feel lucky is to go out of your country and visit places like India, Africa, South-East Asia and South America, and you will see the kind of poverty that exists for so much of humanity.

The country of our birth and its economic conditions are also not of our own doing. We might not be aware of how wide the differences can be unless we travel. And when we do, it is likely that a lot of us will feel a lot luckier about our current situations than we do before.

THE DECADE YOU WERE BORN IN

I was lucky to be born in the late '60s in Singapore.

Singapore gained its independence only in 1965. When I graduated from university in 1992, only 6 percent of Singapore's population were university graduates, compared to about 30 percent today. The number was small because the school system in Singapore kicked into gear only in the late '70s and early '80s. Most of the people who were born earlier than me simply did not have the chance to get an education, even if they were innately very smart.

Singapore was still experiencing tremendous economic growth when I graduated, and I was among a small number of people who had university degrees. So the odds of success for the graduates in my cohort were very good.

Compare this to the young people who were born in the '80s in Spain. When they started coming onto the workforce in the late 2000s, which was when a massive recession happened, they ran smack into a 40 percent youth unemployment rate that persisted *for a decade.* Many of those who got jobs worked below their education level, and many others had to leave the country to find work. *It wasn't anything that they did.* They just happened to graduate during the worst recession the human race has seen since the Great Depression.

Few of us think about the historical context of our births and attribute our success to our own abilities. But when we are older and we look back, it is clearer to us the luck that we had.

WHY IT MATTERS: IF YOU WERE BORN LUCKY

By now, you should realize that luck has a much bigger role in your life than you previously thought. The country you were born in, your birth order, how you look, who your parents were, your innate abilities, your health, and even the decade you were born in had important impacts on your life. You didn't have anything to do with these things, yet they contributed significantly to who you are right now.

The following are why it matters that you know how lucky you already are.

A sense of perspective. Economic and psychological studies have shown that how rich or poor you feel is relative: it depends on how rich or poor the rest of the people around you are. If they are better off than you, you will feel poor, even when on a national or global level, you may be quite well off.

I've heard rich people say they are poor. They do not mean they are poor in an absolute sense but that they are not as rich as the people they know. It can be quite funny when you hear a rich man say, "How can I be considered rich when my yacht is smaller than his!"

If you want to feel the luck you have, one of the ways is to make friends from around the world. Travel to India, China, Africa, Southeast Asia, and South America, and you will see how people around the world live. You will have more people to compare with, and you will gain a more balanced perspective. Another way is to reduce the comparisons you make with the people around you, particularly your friends and family. They have their lives, and they want to live a certain way. You have yours, and you have to march to the beat of your own drum.

I find having the global perspective very liberating. It made me realize that I can live on very little. I don't really need many of the things people are chasing. Hence, I can devote my mind, energy, and cash to the kinds of things I want to do.

<u>A sense of humility.</u> Many people who are successful attribute all their success to their skills and abilities. When asked about their success, they will talk about their brilliant insights and their superb execution. Few will say, "I was lucky." When you have a sense that you were born into many advantages, you will develop a sense of humility. You may see that others who are not doing as well as you were not born with the same advantages. At the very least, you should develop a sense of gratefulness, which is a key ingredient of happiness and contentment in life. If you want to do more, you can help those who are less advantaged.

<u>Sharpening what you have.</u> You'll lose what you don't use. For example, you may have been born with great potential in sports, but if you don't develop that part of you, you will not amount to much. But genes are so powerful that even when you do little, you might still outperform your friends and colleagues in sports; it's just that if you do not push yourself to the limit, you will not see the full extent of what you can do. You might have been able to compete at the national or Olympic level, but you will never know. That's OK if you are doing something else that

you are talented in and love. But it will be a real waste of natural luck if you do not develop what you have an innate potential for and choose instead to do other things you are not so good at.

WHY IT MATTERS: IF YOU ARE NOT BORN SO LUCKY

If you are not born with many of the above lucky situations, this is why it matters:

Knowing your situation and doing something about it. Before reading this chapter, you may not have been aware that you are in a position of disadvantage not of your own doing. But having a greater awareness now enables you to do something about it. There are some things you can change if you want to. For example, you may not belong to the majority race of the country you were born in, but you can move to another country where racism isn't such a big issue or where you actually do belong to the majority race.

Recently, I wrote an article for an online magazine that talked about when it was wise to take a loan from a bank. The principle I gave was that whatever a person wanted to borrow money for should increase his ability to create value for him or herself over time. Taking a loan for a university education is a great example because it increases the person's ability to earn more income over the course of his or her lifetime.

An item that surprised people who read the article was plastic surgery. I said that taking a loan to go for plastic surgery could make financial sense if it would give borrowers greater confidence in themselves and hence increase their odds of success in life. This is especially so if there are physical features that the borrowers may be self-conscious about and lose confidence over. Correcting that feature with plastic surgery could see a surge in such individuals' confidence and cause them to interact with people more.

Turn it to your advantage. For example, fewer women make it to corporate boards than men. This can be seen as a disadvantage because there is a bias against women, or it can be seen as an opportunity. You can work hard to promote the idea of more female representation on corporate boards and raise your profile that way, or you can pitch your credentials to certain boards you know are more open to women.

Work harder. You can curse the Fates and wonder why you were not born with more advantages, but what will that do? Life is unfair; get over it. If you are very clear about what you want in your life and you are able to put tremendous Positive Energy behind your goals, you are likely to still achieve them. The fact that it will take greater effort for you than someone with better advantages should be seen as a good thing. The extra work you have to put in will make you sharper and tougher.

Famous people who succeeded despite the bad luck that they were born with include Stephen Hawking (ALS), Thomas Edison (partial deafness), Helen Keller (blindness), Stevie Wonder (blindness), and John Nash (schizophrenia).

INTERGENERATIONAL LUCK

Charles Darwin observed that finches (birds) in different islands had different lengths of beaks. Those that lived on islands that had more cacti developed longer beaks in order to pick the seeds off the fruit of the cacti. Those that lived on islands where there were fewer cacti developed a taste for small bugs and lived closer to the ground. These developed short, tough beaks in order to catch and crush the insects. Modern-day scientists have even been able to isolate the genes responsible for the lengths of beaks in finches.

Like the animal species around us, we also adapt to our environment. When we do so, we alter our genes and pass them on to our future generations. If they also face the same environmental stimuli, they will continue with the adaptation and make it even more pronounced when they pass on the genes to their offspring.

The most obvious manifestation of human adaptation we can see is skin color. This is a function of where our ancestors lived. Those who lived nearer the equator developed darker skins than those who lived farther away from the sun.

Scientific studies have shown the power of heredity in genes. A lot of who we are, such as our temperament, innate abilities, intelligence, and even our susceptibility to certain diseases, is determined by our genes.

On the good side, we see good qualities being transmitted, like strength and innate skills. For example, Laila Ali, daughter of heavy-weight boxing champion Muhammad Ali, is also a boxing champion in her own right with her WBC, WIBA, IWBF, and IBA female super middleweight titles. On the bad side, research has shown that a mother who smokes has a greater chance of causing her children and grandchildren to develop asthma. This suggests that successive generations of smokers will give rise to offspring with weaker lungs who are more susceptible to associated diseases.

So this is how luck is transmitted through the generations. Your ancestors passed on genes to you that were a function of the environment they lived in and the activities they participated in. You, in turn, influence the genes you pass on to your offspring by your lifestyle choices and what you invest your time and effort in doing.

It is important to know and understand this so you can do something about what you have inherited. For example, with gene testing becoming more and more prevalent, it is possible for you to discover your genetic susceptibility to certain diseases. This is especially important if you know your family has a history of a particular disease. With this knowledge you can better manage your life.

More important is how you choose to live your life that will affect the genes your offspring receives. You can be like Muhammad Ali and pass the strong genes to your children, or you can be a smoker mum who passes on defective genes.

The "luck" in the lives of your offspring is influenced by what you do. Your children will not be very lucky if they are born with asthma and other associated diseases. They will have to spend time, effort, and money to deal with the ailments, which will take their focus and drive away from more productive things.

HOW YOU PLAY YOUR HAND

Life is more like a game of poker than a game of chess.

In a game of chess, it's 100 percent skill. If you're a casual player and you go up against a grandmaster, there is no way you can win. You would lose every game. But in poker, even if you play against the best players in the world, there is still the possibility that you might win because you are dealt a great hand. This is something beyond anybody's control. It's pure luck. Of course, if you learn to play poker well and become greatly skilled at it, your odds of winning will increase.

So it is the same with life. It is part luck, part skills. There's not a lot you can do about the hand you were dealt. This is what you were given. Some were given more, and some were given less. It is not always a good thing to be given more. Sometimes it makes people complacent and lazy, and they simply enjoy what they have without trying to do more. So there's no need to compare with others and wonder why the universe has decided to give you less. Simply accept what you have. Take that as a given. And then move on to do the kinds of things you can do to make your life better.

When I say that life is more like poker than chess, it applies to a single game of poker. In a single game, you might go up against a world champion and still win because you were dealt an excellent hand. But it doesn't apply to one night of three hundred games of poker. If you don't know how to play the game well, you are likely to lose to the world champion in over three hundred games.

It is the same with life. In the short run, you can get lucky. But in the long run, it's your skill and effort that will determine your success.

SCIENCE

There are elements of sociology, evolution, and psychology in this chapter.

The things you were born with will likely define you in the eyes of other people. For example, if you were born rich, other people will see you as rich and want to relate with you that way.

But it is important for your own sense of identity that what you were born with does not define the way you see yourself. You should define yourself by what you choose to do with your life. That's what makes you *you*. You will gain tremendous satisfaction when you know what you have achieved in life is because of the effort you have put in and not merely what you have been given.

You are born with some luck, but it's what
you do with it that defines you.

YOUR GENERATION'S BIG LUCK

*The luck of having talent is not enough; one
must also have a talent for luck.*

—HECTOR BERLIOZ

IF YOU CAN go back to any time in the last fifty years, when would you
go to, and what would you do? Take a moment to think about this, and
write down your answer.

Got it?

I have done this exercise a few times with different people, and I
must say I was surprised that there were a lot more personal situations
than there were financial ones. Many people said that if they were just
given one chance to go back, they would change something personal,
like the choice of a major in college or the relationship with a particular
person. Clearly, for many people, personal matters are more important
than financial ones.

The answers that had to do with money were about buying the lottery or stocks. The favorite stock moments were the stock market bottom
of February 2009, the listing of Apple in 1980, and the return of Steve
Jobs to Apple in 1997.

The last instance is not bad. If you bought shares when Steve Jobs
returned to Apple in 1997, you would have made *three hundred times* your
money by now (in 2017). The market capitalization of Apple was US$2.3
billion in 1997. It is US$800 billion as of this writing in 2017. If you had
invested US$10,000, it would be worth over US$3.4 million.

For me, if I could travel back in time, I would go to Stanford in 1997 and make friends with Larry Page and Sergey Brin. The moment they get the idea to create a new search engine, I would say, "Hey, that sounds like a great idea. I would like to be your first angel investor!" I would be worth billions today.

EVERY GENERATION'S GOLD RUSH

If you were born around the 1800s when human beings first discovered how to harness electricity, you could make a lot of money by making electric things. You could just take anything you see around you at the time and think about how electricity might be added to make it better. One of the most important inventions was, of course, the electric light-bulb because human beings needed light to work at night and in dark places. But after that came the electric coffee percolator, electric lifts, electric fridges, irons, fans, stoves, vacuum cleaners, washing machines, and more. Among the last items was the electric rice cooker, which was invented only in the 1950s by Japanese inventor Yoshitada Minami. He worked with the Toshiba Electric Corporation to produce the first practical electric rice cooker that could be used in the home.

That was the electricity gold rush. People who were involved in businesses that turned what were previously manual, chemical, or mechanical things into electrical ones made a lot of money.

In the '60s, the gold rush for computer hardware began with large mainframe computers like IBM, Digital, and Honeywell. In the late '70s, the personal-computer wave started with people like Steve Jobs and Apple, and now obsolete brands like Compaq, Atari, and Commodore.

In the early '80s, the rush for software gold started, with people like Bill Gates making it big in consumer software and others like Larry Ellison making it big in databases. Lots of other people started smaller software companies to provide niche or customized solutions and made good money. In the '90s, the first wave of the Internet started, with brands like Yahoo and Amazon staking out important spaces. It was also the decade of mobile telecommunication, with brands like Nokia and Motorola leading the trend. In the late 2000s, the trend for app development started, powered by the introduction of the smartphone. A few people made billions from apps, like the founders of Uber, Whatsapp, and Snapchat.

The above examples are mostly tech related, but there are many examples in other fields. For example, anybody who had gotten involved in real estate after World War II would have done well. In the United States, populations tripled from about 125 million to about 330 million in 2017. World populations also tripled from about just over 2 billion in 1945 to 7 billion in 2017. In almost all the major cities of the world, real estate entrepreneurs did very well with the boom in the population.

Other businesses that catered to this huge increase in population also did well. You could be in transport, consumer goods, mining and materials, food, fashion, finance, electronics—the list goes on. Big brands like McDonald's, Coca-Cola, Johnson & Johnson, Boeing, Toyota, Levi's, and many others dominated the global stage.

So with the "go back in time" exercise, if you did some research, you would see there are many periods you could go back to in order to make a fortune. Those periods were the luck that the people from those generations had. Those who acted on their ideas made good money. But those periods are over. It is not possible to make a fortune today from simply making things electric or launching another browser or search engine.

You have to look forward to the gold rush that is happening now or the gold rushes that are coming soon.

WAVES

When a gold rush happens, it may not necessarily be a good thing to be the very first player in the field. The first player usually has to brave tremendous headwinds in dealing with skeptics, bureaucratic officials who are keen to preserve the status quo, and undeveloped or nonexistent infrastructure.

You see it in the early pioneers in frontier land. The first wave of British people who were sent to colonize Australia in the late 1700s or those who ventured to the American West in the early 1800s had a very hard time. So did the first wave of investors who went to China in the early '90s or to Vietnam around the same time. They will tell you they lost a lot of time, money, and effort going around in circles and not being able to get things done.

The second wave is better. The basic infrastructure, systems, and laws are likely to be there. If it's a product, customers have already seen the early versions and got used to the *idea* of the product, even if they are not using it yet. Examples include Google, which we all know wasn't the first search engine. It was not even the second or third search engine. It was something like the ninth or tenth. They basically looked at the weaknesses of the existing engines and built a better one.

Also with Apple when they built the smartphone. They had never made a mobile phone before, and many people thought they would be killed by the likes of Nokia and Motorola, who were the market leaders at the time. But by starting late, they had the opportunity to rethink the mobile phone and incorporate some of the latest technology that was just coming out, like the capacitive touch screens. As we all know, the iPhone went on to become the best-selling phone in history.

In geographical markets, businesses that are now entering Vietnam or China report that they are having a much easier time. Rules are clearer, there is greater respect for copyright protection, and human resources are more abundant.

So when you hear of a new technology, do not fret that you have missed out on the opportunity. It could be a new emerging technology that needs time to mature. There could still be plenty of opportunities to make money.

CAPITALIZING ON MY GENERATION'S LUCK

I was lucky enough to join Procter & Gamble (P&G) in my first job in 1992. It gave me a solid grounding in the things I would do later in life.

I performed well enough at P&G to be promoted a few times in a short few years. When I share with people how I did it, I would point to a few clever things that I did that earned me the promotions.

But there is another telling of the story that greatly minimizes my cleverness. I was simply born at the right time. I was among the first batch of graduates who joined P&G that had a better understanding of how to use computers. If you trace the evolution of the personal computer with my age, you will see that we were some of the first students who got to use computers regularly in school. The IBM XT was the series when I was in university (this was before the Pentium series). My seniors just a few years older than me went through university with little or no computers at all. They were used to doing all their calculations on the calculator.

So when I started work and found that a lot of things were done with pen, paper, and calculators, it was natural for me to initiate some computerization. For my seniors who had no experience of it, it seemed magical that the computer could replace so much of what we were doing by hand, so I was promoted very quickly. How clever was I to notice that processes could be improved with the computer? It was not that much, really. It was obvious to many people my age at the time.

When the Internet wave came in the late '90s, I was thirty years old. It was the perfect age for me and a few friends my age to take advantage of the new technology. We had accumulated some savings and working experience by that point, so we were ahead of the fresh grads. We were also ahead of our seniors, who still hadn't really gotten the hang of working with computers. Many of them didn't even like to type on a keyboard, so they had a much harder time contemplating the implications of the Internet.

So our Internet business became a success. Was it easy to be successful in those days? While we were doing it, it was not clear to us that it was. At the time, there was still a lot of skepticism about the Internet. Access was still via dial-up systems that moved very slowly, and security was always a concern. But as the years went on, broadband came around,

Internet speeds and security got better, and people became very comfortable with performing transactions online.

Looking back, we can see how we got lucky. The initial skepticism kept large competitors out of the game, so we had the time and space to develop our solutions. When the overall infrastructure of the Internet matured, we were at the forefront of our service and product offering.

YOU DO THE BEST YOU CAN, BUT YOU STILL NEED LUCK

You could capitalize on your generation's luck, but it's very hard to say ahead of time which companies will succeed and which will fail. Successful people like to say they listened to their inner voices and went with their gut when they chose a certain route, but there's a lot of "survivorship bias" (an issue described in more detail in the chapter "Lucky Hunches") in these stories. Many more entrepreneurs and others also went with their guts *and failed.* So the fact that many successful people say they owe their success to this and that doesn't mean those things will always lead to success.

Successful people like to make it sound as if their success is due to their own shrewdness, charm, and hard work. These things are indeed necessary, but again, lots of people with those same qualities did not succeed. You can say that those who failed chose the wrong ideas and those who succeeded were smart enough to choose the right ideas, but the reality is that it's not possible to know which idea will succeed at the very beginning, so luck still plays a significant part.

Take Bill Gates for example: When IBM approached him to develop an operating system for a personal computer in 1980, he actually *referred them to someone else!* When that didn't work out, he decided to do it himself, and he became the richest man in the world. Two groups of people at the time didn't think the opportunity would be big: IBM, who could easily have done it themselves, and Bill Gates and his team.

There's also the example from the Google founders, Larry Page and Sergey Brin. One year after starting up Google, *they offered to sell it for*

US$1 million. They couldn't find a buyer, so they decided to do something with it and eventually figured a way to turn it into a US$500 billion company.

Also, look at the venture capitalists. When they invest their money in any idea, all the boxes are checked. They and the entrepreneurs they invest in really do believe the ideas will work. But the result is that the hit rate is very low. Based on available data, they lose money on seven out of ten deals and more or less get back their money on the rest. Maybe one in twenty or thirty ideas results in a big payoff. That's why you will hear that many VCs say they "spray and pray." They invest in as many promising start-ups as possible in the hope of finding a few that will pay off.

The flip side of the story is also interesting. The people at Nokia certainly felt they were invincible in the early 2000s. All the experts in the world did not think Nokia would lose and lose so badly. And remember the Blackberry? Every executive had one, and now it's struggling for survival.

And of course, there's Apple itself. Who thought they would survive their near bankruptcy in 1997 and become the most valuable company in the world? According to the scores of reports written at the time, and even through the early 2000s after Apple had launched the colorful iMacs and the iPod, people were still looking for ways in which Apple would fail. It was only after the middle of 2004 that people started changing their minds and Apple stock started to take off. But the really big idea Steve Jobs had that caused the company to be worth so much today was the iPhone. And the reality is that when Steve Jobs returned to Apple in 1997, he could not have foreseen how Apple would go into the mobile phone business. It was only after Apple developed the iPod Touch that Steve Jobs saw it was a matter of time before all mobile phones were made with the same technology.

So you can't tell right at the beginning. If you are planning to launch an idea, you just have to do your homework and research the idea thoroughly. After that, if your gut feels right, you can decide to go for it and hope for luck. It's not possible to know until you try.

FUTURE GOLD RUSHES

Where are the future gold rushes going to come from?

It's in all the new stuff that people are already talking about: renewable energy, automation, virtual reality, new materials, space travel, and other forward-looking ideas people are discussing. Are you able to get into these ideas? You might think they are too high tech for you, but that would be a misperception.

For example, when electricity first came about, it was also seen as very high tech. But you might not be involved in the implementation of the large electrical generators or the fancy electrical machines. You could have been looking at inventing the electric toaster, which was essentially a few pieces of metal with electricity running through them to heat them up. Or you could have invented or sold the rubber glove to cater to the people who worked with electricity.

It was the same when the Internet first came about. It was very high tech and highly inaccessible at the beginning, but soon the tech became widely available, and people figured out low-tech uses for the Internet and made good money. The invention of Snapchat, for example, had little to do with technology. They used technology that was already available and easily accessible. But they had a unique insight into human nature and created a chat app with functionalities that existing chat apps did not have. It might even seem silly! Snapchat's insight was "ephemeral texting." The idea was that the app would automatically delete users' chats after a few minutes so users needn't worry about their sensitive and potentially embarrassing chats being seen by others. They've developed more sophisticated features since then, but the original big idea was really just that.

Let's look at space travel, one of the most high tech of ideas. There is a space race of sorts by the high-tech companies to make space tourism possible. The idea is to let the man on the street experience space by flying high enough that the spacecraft escapes Earth's gravitational pull and the passengers can experience weightlessness. They can also see the earth as a globe and appreciate the beauty of the planet in space.

At the beginning, this experience will be very expensive, so only the rich people will be able to afford it. But if you imagine forward, you can see a time when the cost will come down and it becomes available to the average person who is planning a vacation. The decision might be, "Honey, should we go to Japan or to space this summer?"

What kinds of things are needed at that time? Space clothes, space luggage, space stickers, space training schools, space souvenirs, space apps, space alumni groups...you can let your imagination soar. What is it you are making right now that can be made for the space consumer?

The above examples are tech related, but there are also important non-tech trends that are underway globally that could present valuable opportunities.

For example, the aging population is one such trend. Human beings are living longer in far greater numbers. What kind of new and unique needs do great numbers of *older* senior citizens have? Rural-urban migration is another important trend. More and more people are moving from small towns to large cities. What kind of challenges will there be and what solutions need to be provided?

BILL GATES' ADVICE

As I am writing this, Bill Gates released a blog post on his website (gatesnotes.com) that is especially suitable for this chapter. First, he talked about how lucky he was to be a part of the digital revolution at the right age:

> *I was lucky to be in my early 20s when the digital revolution was just getting under way, and Paul Allen and I had the chance to help shape it.*

Then he talked about the areas that he would go into if he was in his early 20s today.

If I were starting out today and looking for the same kind of opportunity to make a big impact in the world, I would consider three fields.

One is artificial intelligence. We have only begun to tap into all the ways it will make people's lives more productive and creative. The second is energy, because making it clean, affordable, and reliable will be essential for fighting poverty and climate change. The third is the biosciences, which are ripe with opportunities to help people live longer, healthier lives.

There you have it! This is advice on the next gold rushes, from a man who took advantage of the biggest gold rush of his time.

ONE IMPORTANT CHARACTERISTIC OF BIG IDEAS

If there's one key characteristic to a big idea that you can find, it is this: *few people think it's big at the beginning.* I've already given the examples of Microsoft, IBM, and Google, where even the founders themselves were not sure how big their ideas could be.

Here, I'll reason it out for you. If everybody thinks the idea will be big, then it is too obvious, and a lot of people will be working on them, and usually it is the big companies that will benefit. If nobody thinks the idea will be viable, you also have a problem. It is unlikely you are the only one who can see the opportunity (unless you are the world's foremost expert on the subject).

So the big ideas you can own are the ones that few people think will be big and that you think you have a special insight into or ability for that will make it big. Then, you will be given the time and space to develop the idea without competition from the big companies.

When you have developed it to a significant level, you can form your own company and grow it, like the Google people did, or you can sell your development to a big company that wants it, like the YouTube and Instagram people did.

The point I want to make is that you should be very suspicious if the idea you have is well-liked by everyone you meet. If it is so obvious, it is probably being done by a lot of people; it's just that you don't know about it. I don't want to say that you definitely will not be able to make a success of it. If you think you have a special insight and ability, you can still give it a go. It's just that you have to expect many competitors, and you have to ready yourself for a bloody battle.

The reverse is also important. If you find an idea that few people are looking at, that doesn't mean you will succeed or that it will turn into a big idea. It means only that you are likely to have some time and space to develop it without having to battle many competitors at the same time.

SCIENCE

This chapter is about economics.

The quote at the beginning is from a French musical composer who lived in the mid-1800s and who had a talent for proposing and securing large musical commissions. *"One must also have a talent for luck."* There are plenty of opportunities that the world offers. You should learn to spot them and go after them.

Things are moving faster and faster, and it may be possible for a person to experience several gold rushes in his or her lifetime. The gold rush for electrical products took over a hundred years for everything that can be electrical to be made electrical. For the Internet, it was spread over only about twenty years, and today, just about anything you can put online has already been put online.

There's "gold" in many other fields. You can sit and do nothing and hope that some of that luck coincides with exactly what you are doing, or you can plan for it and go out and start digging.

**Develop a talent for spotting the opportunities
of your time, and take action!**

TAKE ADVANTAGE OF GLOBAL LUCK

*Any fool can have bad luck; the art consists
in knowing how to exploit it.*

—*Frank Wedekind*

On the night of September 11, 2001, in Singapore, I went to bed at 9:00 p.m. because of a cold. My wife also slept early because she was pregnant with our first child. Singapore is twelve hours ahead of New York. If I had stayed up just half an hour later, I would have witnessed the devastation of the terrorist attacks in New York live.

The next morning when I picked up the newspaper, I remember feeling confused as to why the national daily had put some kind of a Hollywood movie on the front page. It took me a while to realize that it was real.

I don't want to be callous about the events of that day. It was a dark day for many people and for humanity as a whole.

But shit happens globally.

And it happens quite regularly. It doesn't matter which decade you look at. There were always man-made disasters like wars, terrorist attacks, and economic crises, and there were always natural disasters like earthquakes, tsunamis, hurricanes, droughts, and diseases.

We can just take the decade of 2000 to 2009, for example. We started the decade with the economic crisis brought on by the dot-com crash in 2000, followed by the September 11 terrorist attacks in 2001, and then we had the Afghanistan war in 2002 and the Iraq war in 2003. In 2003, the world came face-to-face with a new and fearsome disease called SARS. In 2004, a devastating tsunami struck in the Indian Ocean.

The reason I shared that I went to bed early on September 11, 2001, was because it had been a normal day for me, for everyone, before tragedy struck unexpectedly.

So it was with SARS and the tsunami and all the other events. The day before tragedy strikes, everything is normal. But the day it strikes, many things change.

HOW TO MAKE IT WORK FOR YOU

It's bad when these things happen. Lots of people die, and many lives are destroyed. They are tragic events. The world works hard to prevent these events from happening, and a good number can be prevented, but not all. These events will continue to happen in their usual, unpredictable, sometimes inexplicable ways.

I hate to say that we can profit from this, but we can. The idea is to always have some spare cash with you to invest in the global stock markets when these events strike.

If you do not know about investment in the stock markets, you should learn. It will help you increase your wealth. I'm not saying you need to become so good at it that you can trade in the financial markets on a daily basis (unless, of course, you want to make that a career choice). Most people don't need that level of understanding. You just need to know a few things and how to use a few financial instruments when the time is right.

Here, I am going to explain the few things you need to know about investments very simply, and then I'll describe the few financial instruments you can invest in.

IT'S NOT HARD TO UNDERSTAND STOCK INVESTMENTS

Stock markets are formed of companies' shares that are being traded. The very simple thing to remember is that the companies' share prices will go up when their profits go up, and they will go down if their profits go down. (The words "stocks" and "shares" mean the same thing.)

On a daily basis, there are a lot of investors in the stock markets, and some believe that the markets will go up and some that they will go down. That is why there is buying and selling and fluctuation in the share prices.

When disasters such as September 11 strike, global stock markets will go down. The reason this happens is because stock investors will project that companies' abilities to make profits will be severely affected by the event. For September 11, the shares of airline companies went down more than other companies' because investors believed many people would not fly in the following months.

Stock investors also projected that in the aftermath of September 11, more people would stay home out of fear, so shares of retail companies, restaurants groups, and tour operators were hit as well. As such industries are hit, shares of manufacturers of consumer items such as beverages, clothes, electronics, and other things will be affected. These knock-on effects will cause the general stock market across the world to decline.

If you are already heavily invested in the financial markets, you may see the value of your investments go down a lot. If you are invested in big companies (known as blue chips) and you are well-diversified (spread out across many stocks), you can have the comfort that when the crisis is over, the share prices of these companies will come back. If you are invested in small companies, there is a danger that they are so badly affected by the events that they go bankrupt.

So for novice investors, always invest in blue chips.

EXCHANGE-TRADED FUNDS (ETFS)

You need to have a brokerage account with a stockbroker to invest in financial products. The product I am recommending for the general investor to buy is the exchange-traded fund (ETF).

There are many kinds of ETFs. The ones you should know are those that invest in the *large market indices*. In the United States, there are the ETFs that invest in the Standard & Poor's 500 (S&P) Index. This ETF would invest in the top five hundred largest companies in the United States, which would give you a wide diversification across different industry sectors. Most of these companies operate globally, so you are in fact getting exposure to the world. The other ETFs that invest in the Dow Jones Industrial, the Russell 2000, or the Nasdaq 100 can also be considered.

If you do not have access to the US market, you can look at your local stock market and find out about the ETFs that are available. For example, in Singapore we have the ETF that tracks the Straits Times Index. Speak to your financial adviser or stockbroker about the ETFs that track the largest companies in your country.

When disaster strikes, start buying. You will not know when the bottom will be. Sometimes markets can react very quickly and violently and recover just as quickly. Sometimes the markets can slide slowly over the course of a few weeks or months.

At the onset of the tragedy, divide your money into five different equal parts and buy into the ETFs immediately using one part (20 percent). Spread the other four parts over the next two weeks.

Like I said, you are not likely to catch the absolute bottom, but that's not because you are a novice. It's not possible to intelligently pick the market bottom. Many experts will appear on the news to give their opinions, but they are just opinions. Most of them will be wrong simply because the market bottom is a single day out of the many days the markets will be going down. So don't worry about catching that day. If you invest generally during that period, you should get a reasonably good average price.

If you are not confident to do it yourself, consult a financial adviser you trust, and pay him a fee for his advice.

When the markets recover, you should be able to make good profits. In the September 11 crisis, I doubled my money within six months.

HOW CAN YOU BE SURE THE MARKET WILL RECOVER?

The market always recovers. This is because whatever problems the world gets into, human beings always find a way to solve the problems and get back to growth. And when it does and you are invested in the largest companies in the world or in your country, you will do well.

If the world ever gets into a problem you do not think it can solve, you should not invest. But you'd be hard-pressed to say what that event could be. *Wars end, diseases get cured, earthquakes stop, and economic crises recover.* The profitability of the top companies could be affected in the year that the tragedy happens, but their profitability should return to normal a year or two after the event. When that happens, their share prices will return.

But if that is the case, why would people even sell in a crisis?

There are many kinds of investors in the market. There are those who borrowed money to invest, and they are forced to cut their losses to repay their loans. There are those who profit from selling early and look to buying back at a later time when the market has gone down even more (known as short-selling) and these people sell at the first sign of trouble even when they don't own the stocks, which causes prices to plunge. There are those who trade in derivatives, and they are forced to sell when certain pre-set levels are triggered. There are those who sell because the event has affected them personally and they need the money. There are many, many reasons why people sell.

Well-known stock investor Warren Buffet made copies of newspaper front pages reporting on major crises and framed them in his office. He says it's to remind him that catastrophes can occur at any time and without warning. That's why he says he always keeps a significant amount of cash so that he can invest in the markets when disasters strike. When he does commit his cash during a crisis, he will find the most opportune time to sell some of the investments as the markets recover so that he is able to get back to his holding of cash.

And then he waits for the next crisis.

"BLOOD ON THE STREETS"

Baron Rothschild, the eighteenth-century British nobleman banker said:

Buy when there's blood in the streets, even if the blood is your own.

He did so during the panic that came with the Battle of Waterloo against Napoleon, and he made a fortune.

If you follow how Warren Buffet invests, like I do, you will see that he has made obscene amounts of money in crises. Warren Buffet is a legend in the investment community, and many people look to him as a "brand" of confidence. That's why he is able to make incredible deals with companies that need a shot of confidence during a crisis. The companies offer him special deals in their shares because if he takes them, the market will have greater confidence that the companies will survive.

At the top of the financial crisis of 2009, Warren Buffet made sweet deals with Bank of America and Goldman Sachs. The shares he bought at that time have gone up more than four times as of 2017.

SCIENCE

This chapter is about financial investments.

It might seem like bad karma to profit from tragedy. But the human race has always had wars, diseases, and other crises, and it will always have them. Remember that you are not making money from the people directly affected by a crisis—that would be bad karma. You are making money from companies, investors, fund managers, and everybody involved in the investment game.

If you feel bad, you can always donate a portion of your profit to help those who are directly affected by the crisis at hand.

There is luck in crisis.

PART III

LUCKY
MIND-SET

KNOW THE ODDS AND HOW TO BET

*If you drill down on any success story, you always discover
that luck was a huge part of it. You can't control luck,
but you can move from a game with bad odds to one with
better odds. You can make it easier for luck to find you.*

—SCOTT ADAMS

To MAXIMIZE LUCK, you need to understand mathematical probabilities. For those of you who are good at math, you already know this, but you should still read this chapter because I test you with some questions.

For those of you who are not mathematical, don't worry; the math is very simple. You will be able to understand the thinking very easily.

THE COIN TOSS

We'll start with the coin toss. What's the probability of a coin toss coming up heads or tails? It's 50 percent; everyone knows this. This is unless the coin is rigged to come out one way more than the other. However, we won't deal with rigged coins here. All coin examples used here are coins that you brought yourself, and you are 100 percent sure they are fair coins.

Now, if I asked you to place a $100 bet on a coin toss, and I told you that if you got it right, I would pay you $100, and if you got it wrong, you would just lose your $100 bet, would you do it?

Situation 1:
Bet $100, win or lose $100.

You might consider the possibility of losing $100 for a while, but it is something you can think about because the odds are fair.

But if I said that I would pay you only $95 if you won on your $100 bet, would you do it?

Situation 2:
Bet $100, win $95, but lose $100.

You are likely to say no, since it doesn't look fair.

Now, what if I said I would pay you $105 for every time you got it right, and you would just lose the $100 when you got it wrong? What would you do?

Situation 3:
Bet $100, win $105, but lose $100.

You would take the bet, since it sounds like a good deal.

Now, even more interestingly, what if I were to tell you that I'd pay you $105 for every bet you got right and that I would happily go on doing this for one hundred days nonstop, with pauses only for essential functions like sleep, food, and toilet? You would need to put up a minimum capital of $500,000, but there was no limit; you could go on betting even if you lost the initial $500,000.

Situation 4:
Put up capital of $500,000.
Bet continually for a hundred days.
Every bet $100. Win $105, but lose $100.

What would you do?

Most nonmathematical people would make an emotional decision and focus on the areas that give them the most concerns, such as "Where am I going to get the $500,000?" or "It's too troublesome for me to raise the money," or "If I lose $500,000, I'm going to be in big trouble."

But a mathematical person would jump on the bet. He would go and beg and borrow the $500,000, take a second mortgage on his house if he needed to, but he would take the bet for sure. That's because he can be very confident of winning a good amount of money.

How much can he win? This is how you calculate it. The odds of winning are 50–50. So it depends on how many bets are made in the three months. Let's assume it is 200,000 tosses. He should win half the tosses, which would give him $10,500,000. He should lose half of the tosses, which would cost him $10,000,000. The net amount he would make is $10,500,000 minus $10,000,000, which is $500,000. The bettor would basically have an advantage of 5 percent, so you can see that $500,000 is 5 percent of $10,000,000.

A nonmathematical person would ask, "How can we be so sure that the coin tosses will end up with half of them heads and half of them tails? What if I keep betting heads and it keeps coming up tails?"

This is where an understanding of the law of large numbers comes in.

LAW OF LARGE NUMBERS

There is a principle in mathematics called the law of large numbers, which says that given enough instances, the occurrence of events should be very close to its calculated probabilities.

So, with a small number of instances, say 10 coin tosses, it's hard to be confident about how many heads and tails there would be. Even though the odds are 50–50, it doesn't mean that in a small number of tosses, 5 heads would come up and 5 tails. It would be a rather strange situation if it did. Let's say you've had 9 tosses, and you have had 5 tails and 4 heads. If the odds were perfectly correct all the time, this would mean that the last toss *must* be heads. But the last toss has a 50–50 chance of coming up heads or tails, so there is no guarantee it will be heads.

But when the numbers get large, like around 100 tosses, the variance should narrow. You might see 44 heads and 56 tails. And when it gets even larger, like 200,000 tosses in our example above, the instances of heads and tails will be very close to 50–50.

Knowing this in theory is fine, but you really have to experience it in order to increase your understanding of it. If not, your emotions will always take over. For example, if you agree to the 100–105 bet example above, you might be quite happy initially that you have superior odds. But let's say when the coin tossing starts that the first 10 tosses come up tails when you have bet heads and you lose $1,000. And then let's say I offer you a way out, saying, "Looks like Lady Luck is not on your side today. I'm happy to offer you a way out, and you can stop the betting right now." What would you do? Stressed from losing $1,000 so quickly, you might be tempted to give up and take your losses, but that would be a mistake.

Remember that in all our examples, you brought the coin, and you are 100 percent certain it is not rigged. The right thing to do is to keep betting, endure all losses in the short term, and let the law of large numbers work itself out. If you keep going, the odds will play out, and you will win very close to the amount of $500,000 after 100 days.

It is important that you have this understanding of how odds work and don't let your emotions get the better of you. I'll give you real-life examples of how to make the right decisions using odds later in the chapter. The next thing we need to examine is your mind-set on odds.

YOUR MIND-SET AND ODDS

In the coin toss examples above, the odds are fixed. The odds of winning a coin toss are 50–50, and you would only win in the long term if the payout is tilted in your favor. If the payout is even, you would not expect to make any money in the long run because the number of heads and tails coming up is likely to be the same.

Now, let's think about what happens if you increase your odds. Let's take a box and fill it with 100 white ping-pong balls and 100 black ping-pong balls so we know the odds of picking out a black ball or a white ball from the box is 50–50.

What if before you start to pick, I let you make any modifications you want to the box, and you can bet any amount you want on picking a black ball, but you cannot change what is already inside the box. What would you do?

You should find out how many black balls the box can contain, go out and acquire that number of black balls, and put them inside the box. Let's say you found out that the box can contain 800 more black balls, and you put them inside the box, so now there is a total of 900 black balls in the box and 100 white balls. You now have a 90 percent chance of picking up a black ball.

And then I say to you, "Bet on picking the black ball and I'll give you even money. You can bet any amount you like, and when you get it right, I will pay you the amount that you bet. If you get it wrong, I will just take the amount that you bet and nothing more."

What would you do?

Situation 5:
900 black balls and 100 white balls in a box.
You can bet any amount on picking a black ball.
I will pay you the amount you bet if you get it right.

Think.

If I were you, I'd go to my bank, withdraw all the money my bank had, and bet on black. You might say, "Whoa, that's a lot of money! What if the ten percent chance happens and you pick a white ball?" If that happens, I will lose all the money I had in my bank.

My thinking is this: *we don't get many shots at 90 percent odds in life.*

Your question is valid because most people will not take that risk. They want for the box to be filled with 100 percent black balls before they will bet all the money in their bank. Therein lies the problem. There are no certainties in life. If you wait for 100 percent certainty before you make a big bet, you won't achieve much. *If luck has already created a situation that is highly advantageous to you and you still cower from making the big bet, how are you going to make it big in life?*

If you bet everything you had and you were unlucky and picked a white ball, you could tell yourself that you were unlucky, go back to work, and make back the money that you lost. But if you bet a little money and a black ball came up, and the odds had been very high that it would, you would curse yourself forever for not betting everything you had on something that was 90 percent.

A BIT MORE ON ODDS

We are still on the box with the 900 black balls and the 100 white balls. What if I told you that instead of one bet, you can make two bets. What would you do? With two bets, you can increase the odds of winning and at the same time diversify your risk substantially.

What should you do with the two bets? You should go home, take all the money out from your bank, borrow all you can, sell all your possessions, and muster all the money you can in the world, and then come back and split the money you have into three parts. Let's say the total you can muster is $1,500,000, so each part is $500,000.

The way you should bet is one part on the first bet, so $500,000 on the first bet. If you win, you can walk away because winning one-third of the value of all your possessions in the world is already quite good. The odds of the second bet are still quite good, at 90 percent for black, so you can bet another $500,000 if you like, or you can bet less. If you win, it will be another $500,000. If you lose, your total winnings from the two bets will be the winnings from your first bet minus the loss from your second bet.

Now, what happens if you really have bad luck and you pick a white ball and lose the first bet? You should take all the money you have left, which is $1 million, and bet it all on black. The odds of picking two white balls are 0.1 x 0.1, which is 1 percent, meaning the odds of having *at least one black ball* in two bets in a box where 90 percent of the balls are black go up to 99 percent.

Now, the odds of the second bet *itself* are still 90 percent. It is no different from the first bet, but the difference between being given one bet and two bets is that the odds of having at least one of the bets come out as black has gone up significantly from 90 percent to 99 percent. *You basically have two chances of going at something that is 90 percent.* With such odds, it should justify selling all your possessions and making the bets.

Even as I say this, there will be people who will say, "I will never sell all my possessions and bet on anything, no matter how good the odds are." Even when the odds are at 99 percent! Think about what your position is. Not what your mind says but what your heart says. Your mind might say, "Yes, the odds make sense," but in your heart you might think, "I'll never do it, no matter what the odds are."

Of course, nothing in life can give 99 percent certainty, so this exercise is partly to help you learn how to calculate the odds and partly to test you on your tolerance of risk. *If you are not a risk-taker at any level of risk, you may not benefit much from the luck you get in life.*

WHEN ODDS ARE BAD

I don't want to seem like I am overselling risk-taking. It's about the odds. Go big on the risk-taking only if the odds are great. What if the odds aren't so good? Let's go back to the coin toss and the $100 bet. Let's say I pay you only $95 when you get it right, and you lose $100 when you get it right. Should you do it? Of course you shouldn't.

But let's say I entice you with three free bets, where if you win, you keep the $95 from each free bet, and when you lose, you lose nothing. What would you do? Take the bets, of course; they are free! Let's say you win all three free bets and you've won $285, and then I suggest we do it where you win $95 on a $100 bet. What would you do?

If you're really in that situation, you might feel quite lucky from winning the free bets and decide to carry on betting. You will think you can afford to lose up to $285 since that is money you have already won. But the right thing to do would be to walk away and not make the bets at all. You shouldn't take bets you know are unfair against you, no matter how "lucky" you feel.

Do you think this situation is so obvious that I needn't have posed the question? Well, have you ever gambled at a casino before? In all the games in a casino, the odds are roughly 5 percent in favor of the house. *When you gamble in a casino, you are really placing $100 bets and winning only $95 because that's how the odds are set up.*

Yet many people do that. Many do so because they think it is a dalliance with Lady Luck or a battle with fate. But it's neither. In the long run, you will always lose. I talk more about gambling in the chapter called "Gambling Luck."

IT MAY NOT SEEM LIKE BAD LUCK WHEN YOU HAVE MORE INFORMATION

Let's say you drive into a parking lot and see the car in front of you take the very last available place. You may say, "Oh, I'm so unlucky to be the one after the last place is taken!" And then you might decide you want to exit and drive to another parking lot farther away.

But you should stop and ask yourself what more information about this parking lot you can get. Suppose you find a blog post online that says the people who park here are mainly just running to the ATM and that most cars are parked only for three minutes on average. What would you do? You might decide to wait three minutes for someone to leave than to go to another parking lot farther away.

Additionally, you might turn to whoever is in your car with you and say, "Hey, I bet you guys ten dollars that we will get a parking lot space within the next three minutes." Your friends might see that the parking lot is full and take the bet.

When you win the bet, your friends may say, "Man, you just got lucky because that lady came out to get her car." And you can reply, "Yeah, I'm lucky!" But really you're not. You just had superior information on the bet.

REAL-LIFE EXAMPLES

The first time my wife got pregnant, we had a miscarriage in the fourth week. Now, a lot of people who face such a misfortune may say, "Oh, how unlucky I am!" and start to think about the various sins they have committed in the past and wonder if the misfortune was karmic payback for those sins.

But when we did a bit of research, we found that 30–50 percent of all pregnancies are lost within the first few weeks. Most women don't even know they are pregnant or are having a miscarriage and just think it is a delayed period that has come with a heavier flow. It's the body's natural way of getting rid of a pregnancy that was somehow not right. That's why doctors advise people to hold off announcing their pregnancies until after the first trimester is over. My own mother then shared with us that she experienced the same thing when she had been trying to conceive for the first time.

When we discovered it was a natural thing that occurred in such high frequency, we no longer thought of ourselves as unlucky. Since the odds are up to 50 percent, which is very high, it is no surprise that it happens. Our feelings of sadness went away immediately. Soon after, my wife conceived again and we had our first son, followed by another son three years later.

I think we are very lucky to live in the age of information, when data, knowledge, news, personal accounts, and other types of information can be easily gotten. If we had lived in an earlier time, the miscarriage might have been attributed to some kind of supernatural action or divine punishment.

Lots of people also suffer from depression, sadness, anxiety, or a sense of helplessness about life, and they think they are so unlucky to be the only ones going through their sufferings when their friends all look like they are having such great lives. But the reality is that everyone is struggling with something at some point in time, and now it is easier to read about those conditions online and find support. If you do a bit of research on the subject, you might find that a lot of other people have the same experiences and challenges as you, and there are many places to find help.

If you are in such a situation, just knowing that many others are likely going through the same thing as you should make you feel better. You are not unlucky. When a lot of people are going through the same thing, it really is just a passage in life, so don't feel bad!

To discover whether the odds are in your favor, sometimes you need to do some work and get more information. *Do not just sit there and mope about how unlucky you are!* What appears to be daunting challenges against you could actually be very common when you have more information. You might even find a way to turn that situation to your favor.

GREATER ODDS IN LIFE

Real-life opportunities don't come with labels that say what their probabilities of success are. You have to gauge them yourself. I have seen tremendous opportunities in my life that have greater than even odds of success, and I have capitalized on them.

Investing in the stock markets. I know that a lot of people think it is very complicated, but it is actually very simple. Stocks of companies go up when they make more profits, and the more people there are in the world or a country, the more people need to buy stuff made by the companies, and the more their profits go up. That's all!

So the last seventy years have been a great time to buy stocks. The world's population was at about 2.5 billion after World War II, and it has now grown to over 7 billion. It is projected to grow to 9 billion in 2040.

We see the same tremendous growth in the United States after World War II. It had about 130 million people then, and it has 330 million now.

US companies who catered to their home market have mostly done very well, and their share prices have gone up. All you had to do was buy a US Index fund, and you would have made good money.

Investing for the long term in a large market like the United States or investing in a globally diversified portfolio of stocks is a way of making money that has great odds. *You already know that world populations will rise.* It means there will be more people who will buy more products and increase the profits of the companies that make those products. As their profits rise, so will their share prices.

<u>Growth industries</u>. Are you a young person looking for a job with good prospects? You should join a company in a growth industry rather than one in a sunset industry. The likelihood of you getting pay increases and promotions in a company in a growth industry will be a lot higher.

You don't know whether the job you're in is in a growth industry or not? Do some research and try to get more information. You might be in a sunset industry. You can't say, "Oh, I'm so unlucky to be retrenched," when you have never tried to find out more about the industry you're in.

<u>Jobs availability</u>. Do you live in a small town where the good jobs are few? Your odds will greatly improve if you move to a big town or large city where the jobs are plentiful.

<u>Finding a significant other</u>: Are you looking for a potential mate? The more dating websites you join, the more gyms, singles' clubs, and community events you go to, the greater your odds of finding someone.

SCIENCE

This chapter is mainly mathematics. It's important to have a good sense of the odds so you know how to take appropriate risks and not let emotions cloud your judgment. If you insist on certainty in life, you will not do well. If you take too much risk when the odds are against you, you will also not do well.

To have a better sense of the odds in real life, it's often necessary to get more information about the situations you are in. With more information, some situations might look better and others worse. You can then make the appropriate decisions.

Do not blame everything on luck when you have not done the work to improve your odds. For example, I've met single people who simply expect that love will happen miraculously without much effort on their own. Their reasoning is, "If it is meant to be, it will come." That kind of thinking does not work at all! If you want it, you have to put yourself in a situation where the odds of you getting it are high.

Develop a sense for the odds, gather more information, and bet according to the risks.

THE TEMPLE OF LUCK

Leave all the afternoon for exercise and recreation,
which are as necessary as reading. I will rather say more
necessary because health is worth more than learning.

—THOMAS JEFFERSON

THE TEMPLE OF luck is your body. You have to take care of it and keep it in top condition.

To start, I'd share with you one idea that you may not be familiar with. It is this: We don't have to eat three meals a day. Scientists and nutritionists say that there is no magic to the number three. It can be more or it can be less. It all depends on how much energy we need in the day. If we lead a largely sedentary lifestyle, consisting mostly of going to work, typing on keyboards and coming back home, having three large meals could be too much for our needs.

Along with this, the idea that breakfast is the most important meal of the day is also wrong. Scientists have reported that there is scant evidence to support this and have suggested that the idea may have been promoted by breakfast cereal companies in order to sell more of their products.

It is my opinion that the idea of having a large breakfast and the idea of eating three meals a day have led to the high rates of obesity in much of the developed world.

WE ARE OVEREATING

A few years ago, I started skipping breakfast. I chose to skip breakfast because it was the meal that I had most control over. I often have lunch with colleagues and clients, and dinner with family, so it's hard to skip those.

It was tough in the first week or so because my body was used to getting food, but after that it was OK. I ate a normal lunch and then half a dinner. I lost 10 kg over three months, and then it became stable after that. I'm at 70 kg, which is ideal for someone who is 178 cm in height.

Skipping breakfast means that my body doesn't get any food for about eighteen hours. It's a daily fast that lasts from dinner at 7:00 p.m. to lunch at 1:00 p.m. the next day. If you google "benefits of fasting", you'll see that fasting promotes weight loss, lower blood pressure, and reduced cholesterol. There is also a cellular process called autophagy, where the body cleans waste products that are left by dead and damaged cells, that has many health and antiaging benefits.

Of course, this is not for everyone. If you are below eighteen years of age, you need a lot more calories because you are growing and likely to be physically active. Also, if you have certain health issues, you should take the advice of your doctors.

But my point for you to consider is that we in the first world are overeating. We are still eating the same amounts as our forefathers when they were in the fields. Now that we are in the office, it's way too much. We should eat according to what we need and not allow our bodies to store too much excess energy in the form of fat. And we should consider fasting periodically to let our bodies cleanse themselves.

WE ARE MALNOURISHED

How can we be overeating and malnourished at the same time? We can if our meals are unbalanced and filled with processed foods. You can google "types of processed food" for a full list. Processed foods are filled with lots of unhealthy and unnatural chemicals that are not nutritious and are known to cause cancer.

Anything that is fresh, natural, and cooked simply is the best. Some say it is expensive to eat this way, but not if you reduce the quantity. You should find out the amount of calories you need to get you through your day and eat according to that. You might find that this is a smaller amount than what you eat now.

So you can decrease the quantity and increase the quality. When you are better nourished, you will be more alert, and your body will feel better, ready for whatever life has to offer you.

WE ARE SUNLIGHT-DEFICIENT

Many of us could be getting too little sun. (I say this generally because those of us living in the tropics often think we are getting too much of it). Scientists tell us that moderate exposure to sunlight lowers blood pressure, cleans the blood and blood vessels, enhances the body's ability to deliver oxygen to the tissues, helps with stamina and muscular growth, and helps build and strengthen the immune system.

What might be less known is that sunlight improves your sex life as well by converting high cholesterol into sex hormones. Sunlight also cures and prevents depression. If we are out of the sun, we can become prone to a condition called Seasonal Affective Disorder and grow sad and depressed.

But overuse of sunblock can lead to many problems, including, as some reports suggest, cancer. So plan to go out into the sun, but limit the exposure so you don't need to use sunblock.

WE DON'T HAVE ENOUGH EXERCISE

You've probably heard a lot about the benefits of exercise so I don't need to talk too much about it. I just want to share that almost all the top leaders I know have an exercise regimen. They say that if they don't exercise, they won't have the required energy to get them through their demanding jobs. Some of them are very fit and are able to run marathons. But others simply have a regular regimen they can do comfortably, like going for swims or walks. Just doing something simple can give a big boost of energy, as opposed to doing nothing at all.

I've talked about energy throughout this book, and exercise is the thing that will give you more energy and stamina. If you don't exercise, you will find that your energy through the day doesn't last very long. You will feel tired easily. Even when you don't do much, you will feel very lethargic. When your physical body is in that state, it will tell your mind not to do stuff. Consequently, you will become less active, and you will achieve less.

HEALTH DISCRIMINATION

Directly related to the topic of luck is the issue of health discrimination. The world is becoming more equal. We are learning *not* to discriminate by gender, race, nationality, or age. But there's evidence that we continue to discriminate against a person's health.

Here are some common types of health-related discrimination.

Physical and psychological health discrimination. If you have physical health issues such as hypertension, cancer, high blood pressure, and substance abuse, or psychological health issues, such as chronic or acute depression, anxiety, and psychological distress, you may find that you cannot get a job or that you are passed over for a promotion and other opportunities.

The reason is simple: people around you will think you don't have the ability to assume those responsibilities.

If your health issues are hereditary, you don't have a choice: you simply have to learn to manage them. But if they are there because of your lifestyle, you can do something about it.

Smoking Discrimination. Global smoking rates are coming down. In the United States, the percentage of US adults who smoke cigarettes has declined to 16.8 percent as of 2014. In Australia, the number is down to 13.3 percent as of 2013, and there has been some talk that when the rate goes down to 5 percent, cigarettes will be banned altogether.

It is well documented that there is discrimination against people who smoke. It can be official discrimination, such as when laws are enacted to restrict the ability of smokers to smoke in various places. Or it can be employer discrimination, if they think that a smoker will offend clients or that the health insurance costs will go up.

There is also social discrimination. As more and more literature is emerging that second- and third-hand smoke (the smoke that lingers on a smoker's body) can have adverse effects on those surrounding the smoker, it is only natural that nonsmokers would shun smokers.

The numbers are against the people who smoke. If we take the 2014 number in the United States, it means that for every seventeen smokers, there are eighty-three nonsmokers, so the nonsmokers will be a more powerful group that will continually ask for protection against smokers.

Obesity Stigma and Bias. It's tough being too fat. The world is designed for the average person, so a large person will find many inconveniences, such as when airplane seats and toilets seats are too small. More dangerous will be when the medical supplies and equipment in the country cannot fit those who are too large.

Again, there may be employer discrimination because of concerns over performance as well as higher insurance costs. The social discrimination is probably the worst. When friends or acquaintances make fat jokes, the large person just has to take it in, or else he or she will be seen as not being a good sport. A lifetime of jokes, pranks, and insults can have very damaging and lasting effects on the large person's psychology.

Some people are born large but are fit and healthy, such as Asian action star Samo Hung, who is large and round but who can still perform acrobatics and fight. If you fall into this category, you have to demonstrate to those around you that you are large *and* fit, and the discrimination should lessen or stop.

But if you are large because you overeat, you will find that others around you will not share opportunities with you. They will assume you have self-control and health issues.

Consequently, your luck will not be very good.

ALERTNESS AND CREATIVITY

In an earlier chapter, I said that luck comes from ideas. To get the best ideas, your mind must be clear and alert. If it is constantly numbed by food, alcohol, or lack of sleep, it cannot perform at its best.

To perform at its best, the brain needs fresh food and regular exercise. We all know the effects of fatty and oily foods on our physical and mental performance. We feel lethargic and dazed. For example, you cannot have a proper brainstorming meeting after a heavy lunch of oily and fatty foods.

But lean meats, fresh fruits, and vegetables keep us alert and energetic. Research has shown that exercise leads to faster neural conduction between brain regions and superior thinking and memory performance. Conversely, lack of exercise can change the brain negatively, with some studies showing that it can lead to brain shrinkage in middle age.

Overall, if the people around you see that you are often dazed, hungover, or slow to think and remember things, you will be labeled as a nonperformer and passed over for opportunities.

COMBINING PHYSICAL ACTIVITY WITH CREATIVITY ENHANCEMENT

Authors Olivia Fox Cabane and Judah Pollack, who wrote the book *The Net and the Butterfly: The Art and Practice of Breakthrough Thinking*, say that "mindless" activities promote creative thinking.

In an interview in the February 2017 issue of *Fortune* magazine, they said:

"What's the single best mindless activity I can do?" Our clients often ask us. If we had to choose one, it would be walking.

So walking is great. It helps burns calories, puts oxygen into our system, prevents our muscles from atrophying, and also enables us *to daydream and become more creative.*

ALL THINGS NATURAL ARE OK

That's the principle in our household.

The things around us belong to three categories of natural sources. They are animal, vegetable, or mineral. The fourth category is not natural. These are the by-products of petroleum, which are mainly plastics and Styrofoam.

In my household, we avoid all things that are made of plastic and Styrofoam where possible. Our eating utensils are made of wood or metal, our drinking cups are made of glass, and the water bottle we carry out is made of metal. When we put food or drink in these things and they interact with their containers and we get minute traces of glass, wood, or metal in our bodies, it's not a problem because these are natural things our bodies have gotten used to.

It's the plastic and Styrofoam that our bodies have trouble coping with. A few countries have already banned Styrofoam. And classifications of plastics are appearing to tell us which ones are safe to be used with food and drink. But it's still a little confusing, so the mantra in our home is, if we can avoid plastic, we avoid it.

CONCLUSION

The energy we have comes essentially from two sources. The first is psychological. It's our desires, our motivations, and our perceived purpose in life. The second is the physical energy from our bodies. We may have the greatest desire in the world to achieve something, but if our bodily energy is low, we can't do much.

So build greater physical energy for yourself. When you are living a healthy lifestyle and functioning at peak levels, you will feel a profound high similar to the kind athletes get. The people around you will see you glow, and they will be attracted to you.

That's when luck starts to come.

Good luck starts with a healthy and energy-filled body.

MAKE SPACE FOR LUCK

*Truth is ever to be found in simplicity, and not
in the multiplicity and confusion of things.*

—Isaac Newton

THERE CAN BE too much noise and drama in our lives that it clutters up all our mental and emotional spaces. Our minds, hearts, and energies are so completely devoted to managing these things that they are "not available" to see and take on opportunities when they come.

If you are generally feeling stressed, anxious, and confused, your energy is at odds with good luck. You need to deal with these negatives so you can go back to being the comfortable, positive, and creative person you are.

You need to simplify your life. The first thing you can do is reduce the number of things you are involved in. Can you find something you can quickly cancel or quit so you can free up time and mental space? If so, do it.

Now, I'll talk about how you can declutter from some of the seemingly inextricable parts of your life.

DECLUTTER FROM SOCIAL MEDIA

Are you getting offended and hurt by what people are saying about you on social media? This could be from postings you make or from comments you leave on other people's postings. As you probably know, online arguments can get quite bad, and they use up a lot of your attention and energy.

Social media is here to stay, so it's hard to say that you should stop. But if you are getting a lot of angst, you can try "detoxing" from social media for a while, say, a month or so. Just read and not post. With frequent pauses, you will find that you can feel more detached with social media usage and have greater control.

DECLUTTER FROM YOUR PARENTS

Are your parents the source of a lot of drama for you? You could have "overcaring" parents who are still hovering over you like you are a child and telling you what to do all the time. You feel crowded out by their voices and frustrated by their lack of understanding.

The way to manage this is to *not* get into arguments with them. You don't have to try to convince them that you are right. Just listen to what they say, and then smile and say back, "Thanks for your advice," and leave it at that. No matter what they say, do not get drawn into arguments with them, and do not walk away in frustration. Just take it in, smile, and say thanks. It's a neutral response that preserves the relationship without getting yourself drawn into arguments. If they press you for an answer, just give them a kiss on their foreheads and say, "I'll think about it," and walk away.

The idea is to have a neutral, non-emotional response that neither agrees nor disagrees. That is the way to communicate that you value their opinions because they are your parents, but you have to make your own decisions about your life.

DECLUTTER FROM YOUR CHILDREN

I am a parent of teenage kids, and I've read all the psychology literature on managing teenagers. But the best advice I can find comes from the singer Sting in the title of his song: *"If You Love Somebody, Set Them Free."*

If you google you can find many quotations of people across different generations complaining about their young. Every generation thinks it knows better than the next, that "youth is wasted on the young." And yet succeeding generations of human beings have always surpassed previous ones and brought the human race forward.

We need to teach our children important values in life, like honesty and charity, and then we need to let them live their lives and trust that they will do the right things for themselves. Our children need to have their own space to make their own mistakes and to fail. That's the only way they can become wise and resilient. We should hold back our impulses of worry and the need for nagging.

My mantra for my children is, "Always love, and let them be." If you're having too much drama with your children, you can try decluttering this way.

DECLUTTER FROM FRIENDS

Friends are the best and the worst things for you. Friends are the best because they support you no matter what you do. But they can be the worst if you constantly compare yourself to them. If you do that and track who owns what, who did what, who bought what, and who said what, your mind will be filled with needless angst.

Comparing ourselves with others is an evolutionary response for us to check if we have enough resources to survive. It is an innate response that has been coded into our DNA. We do it and are happy when we have more, and we feel envious when we have less. There will be an innate impulse for us to try to acquire the same things our friends have. We have to silence this impulse. It will lead us down roads we don't need to travel.

Be clear about your own path and focus on that. Your friends have their own paths to travel.

DECLUTTER FROM YOU

A lot of the drama in your head is imagined and created by you.

- You reflect constantly on your mistakes.
- You wonder why this or that person is so unfair to you.
- You feel others attacking you.
- You feel the world doesn't understand the things that are important to you.
- You feel the world is against you.

Here's a thought I learned early on that gives me great comfort: *nobody cares about me*. So nobody cares about you. This is not meant to make you sad. It's meant to liberate you. You may think that a lot of people care about a lot of the things you do, but really they are all concerned about themselves and are not paying a lot of attention to you.

You may have failed at something, committed an embarrassing gaffe, fell on your face, said something stupid that went viral on social media, et cetera, and you feel that the whole world is laughing at you. They may do so at the moment the incident happens, but the next day, they go right back to their own issues, their own embarrassing moments, their own gaffes and worries.

They don't really have time to think about you. When others disagree with you, they are *not really disagreeing with you*. They may be worried that *they* are seen as wrong since your viewpoint is different from theirs, and they feel the need to defend themselves. They may have self-esteem issues and an irrational need to always win an argument. They may have been scolded by their bosses just prior to meeting you, and they just want to vent in front of you. Who knows? There's a lot that could be going on in their heads.

Even when they look like they are talking about you, what they are really doing is projecting themselves onto you. It's not about you. It's still about them! So you can't take what are really other people's issues and think they have something to do with you.

Here's an example: When I started skipping breakfast and felt the wonderful benefits of it, I went around telling everyone they could lose some weight by skipping breakfast. After a while, I realized my friends heard it as me calling them fat. But my intention was really to show how clever and self-disciplined I was in skipping breakfast, and I wasn't saying that anyone was fat. I was talking about me, and my friends thought it was referring to them!

So let's do this exercise: Someone says to you, "Why don't you lose some weight?"

In your mind you can think:

- The whole world thinks I am fat and ugly.
- Excuse me; you're not so light yourself, all right?
- Sigh, I really shouldn't have missed my runs last week. I'm so ill disciplined.
- Why does this person always say bad things about me?
- I'm not fat! It's just water retention, all right?

Which thought is the right one?

None of them! That's all drama you can declutter from! Whatever other people say, they are just pieces of information for you. Good or bad, just thank them and move on. They have their own personal reasons for saying what they say, and it has nothing to do with you. So the answer to "Why don't you lose some weight?" is, "Hey, thanks, yeah, I'll look into it." You can stop there, but if you want to make conversation, you can say, "Got any suggestions?" And take whatever the person says as additional information, nothing more.

So all the gaffes, faux pas, mistakes, boo-boos, embarrassments, humiliations, offenses, and so on—declutter your mind from them. Nobody cares. If "nobody cares" sounds a bit harsh, use this phrase instead: *it doesn't matter.*

Put them out of your mind, and go back to your goals.

DECLUTTER FROM STUFF

If you are serious about pursuing your dreams, you are likely to require money to do so. You have to take stock of how you are spending your money right now. The clearer you are about what your true goals are, the less "stuff" you will feel you need. Most of us accumulate stuff because we don't know what else to do. So our minds are open to all the noise that comes at us from advertising and seeing what our friends buy.

The moment our minds are filled with a goal, we will tune out all the marketing noise, and our spending will reduce accordingly. If you are clear about what you want, you will even save up for it, sometimes for years if necessary. You will find that you can get along find with very few stuff.

RESETTING YOUR LIFE

Although I say we need to know what we want so that our lives can be more focused, the reality is that we don't always get it right the first time. In fact, we may not get it right many times! It is perfectly all right to press the reset button and start over.

It doesn't matter if doing so sets you back a few years. Nobody's counting but you, and if you think it's what you want to do, then you should go ahead. At the back of your mind, you may think, "Oh, everybody has already achieved so much, and if I choose to reset my life, I will be so far behind." This is a common thought, and it will linger. Your friends and family may even say similar things to you.

But it's up to you how much weight you want to give to comments and thoughts like this. When your friends and family say these things, they are merely projecting their reality on you and saying that *if* it were them, they would decide a certain way. It's just more information for you to consider. Only *you* are living your own reality, so you have to decide what is good for you. It doesn't matter if it is your sixth reset and you are in your sixties or seventies. It doesn't matter if *you* don't think it matters! That's all that matters!

More importantly, it's not uncommon for people to reset their lives and try something new at an older age. Just google "people who started late" and you will get many inspiring stories of people who found success and their life's calling at very advanced ages. So the idea that once you're a particular age you're supposed to be doing this or that is wrong. You can choose new directions for your life at any time, just as so many successful people have done.

CONCLUSION

The quote at the start of the chapter is from Isaac Newton, a physicist. So I would say that simplicity is a kind of philosophy that cuts across all fields.

It's also an important facet in positive psychology to reduce negativity and simplify your life. You'll find that your bandwidth to do stuff is greatly increased. You can fill the space you've created with lots of positive and creative energy in the pursuit of your goals.

Good luck will find you soon enough.

Your life may be filled with too much unnecessary clutter for good luck to come in.

LUCK TAKES TIME

*If your current get-rich project fails, take what you learned
and try something else. Keep repeating until something lucky
happens. The universe has plenty of luck to go around;
you just need to keep your hand raised until it's your
turn. It helps to see failure as a road and not a wall.*

—Scott Adams

WE HATE TITLES like these.

"Why must it take time? Isn't there a shortcut to luck and success? Isn't that why I would even consider buying this book?" Well, it's different for different people and different ideas. Sometimes it does come very fast; sometimes it takes a while.

INSTANT LUCK

Yeah, now we're talking!

No, we're not. Unfortunately, in my experience, instant good luck is often bad luck. *It comes too easily, and you won't know how to manage it.* You will think you can count on instant luck all the time and not develop any of the coping skills you need in life. That's why many lottery winners will tell you they are miserable and wish they had never won the lottery. You can read more about this in "Lottery Luck."

I've experienced instant luck a few times with my businesses. For example, when we first started our transport business, we got a bus supplier who was the best guy you could ever find. He was dependable, on time, friendly—everything you'd ever want in a bus operator. This made us think that all suppliers were going to be like that, and we built our business around it. Unfortunately, the other bus suppliers we got were a far cry from the first one. The "industry average" of reliability was way below our experience with the first guy. We made a mess of the operations in the next few buses and disappointed many passengers. So we learned the hard way that it's great to get a wonderful supplier, but we have to manage the operations in a way that doesn't depend on that. Wonderful suppliers are a plus, but not the standard.

Sometimes businesses and projects do get instant luck and go on to become huge hits. It's like the movie *The Social Network*, which shows the founding and growth of Facebook. It talks about how Facebook had instant success from day one as a university social network and how it went on to become the global social network for everyone.

These occurrences are very rare (that's why they get made into movies), and when they are talked about a lot, it puts the false idea into people's heads that businesses have to be instant hits or not exist at all.

NORMAL-TIME LUCK

I had a friend who started a business consultancy practice. He was very experienced and knowledgeable in his area, so he was able to attract a few junior associates to join him in his new venture. I was there at the launch, and it seemed like he was off to a good start.

When I bumped into him two years later, I was surprised to hear him say he had closed the business and gone back to work in his old company. He told me he had had great difficulty getting clients, and he just couldn't grow the practice. And then he said, "It was really bad luck too because just after I decided to close the practice, a few large companies called to ask if I could take on a few interesting projects. Well, how was I to know, right?"

I think many people are too heavily influenced by movies like *The Social Network*. But the movie, as well as stories that lucky businessmen tell, really do give a false impression of success. Most of the time, instant luck does not happen, and anything that is worth doing will usually take a much longer time and require a much greater effort. You *might* get lucky, but you cannot *plan* on the luck. Your plan A should be preparing to hunker down for the long haul. If the instant luck comes, that's great. But if it doesn't, you still have a plan to execute.

THE LUCK CURVE

I have been asked by some young entrepreneurs, "I have X dollars to start a business, and I project that I will achieve breakeven in Y amount of time. Is that realistic?" Without looking at what their idea is and how they plan to execute it, I reply, "You need at least three times that amount of money and time." These are young and relatively inexperienced entrepreneurs, of course. If they were experienced, they wouldn't be asking such a question.

The young entrepreneurs' questions are usually based on a projection that looks like line 1 below. They have a straight-line projection upward, and they set aside just enough money for that to happen. In reality, outside of the hits with instant luck, the progress of a business or any worthwhile endeavor is more like line 2.

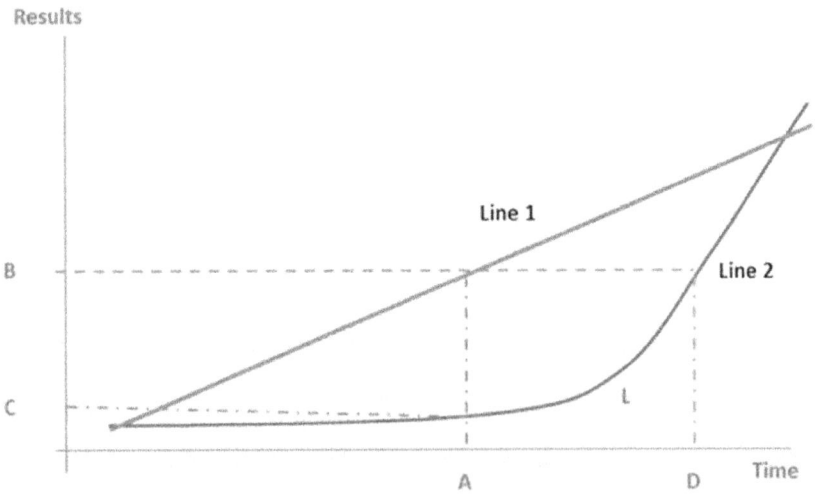

It's actually quite a familiar curve to business students. They call it the j-curve because it is shaped like the letter *J*. In some drawings where the y-axis is labeled as "returns" rather than "results," the curve could dip below the x-axis and show negative returns. This reflects the high costs that new project or business would incur in the early stages.

Despite knowing about the j-curve, however, there is still a persistent desire to create projections that are a straight line like line 1. I think this is because everyone is in a hurry to see good results. But in reality, the j-curve is almost always there. So what happens when time period A is reached is that the people who are working on the project start to panic. They are on point C in results and very far away from point B that they had projected. The panic is especially obvious in bootstrapped companies where the founders are funding the project. It's all the money they have, and they become very unsure about whether to ask friends and family to step in and help.

When the main person in the project starts to panic, the teammates will start to panic. When no one on the team can overcome their fears, they will give up. Line 2 predicts they will give up just when their luck is about to kick in and business is about to start rolling.

Why so? What happens with a new business or a new project is that in the beginning, few people will know about it. The team is likely to struggle with teething issues in the setup of the project. The initial service or product might also not be the excellent service or product the team is capable of because not everything is in place, so the initial customers might not be too happy with it.

Soon, however, if the team is good, they will start to get things working and start delivering at their best. When that happens, they will need to find some new customers because the early ones did not experience the best of what they had to offer. When the new customers discover they are really quite good and use the service or product more and tell their friends about it, that is when the business starts to take off.

The initial stage takes time, effort, and resources, but there won't be a lot of results. So when the initial capital or resources are used up, the team members might start to panic. If that panic is not properly managed, the project will end. It could be a tremendous pity because the turnaround could really be just around the corner. The word of mouth from clients might just be starting to spread. The suppliers might just be starting to become familiar with the management team and willing to give better terms. Someone out there might just be learning about the project and planning to suggest a partnership.

Businesses and projects that give up too early never get to find out all the amazing luck that's coming up.

"BUT HOW DO YOU KNOW WHEN TO STOP?"

This is a question I get very often. I say, "Persevere," and many people will ask how they will know if it is time to quit.

You have to examine the basic premises you had when you first started the project. Are the premises still intact? For example, if you went into a baking business because your friends and family believe that no one else in the world can bake as good as you and you have absolute confidence in your cakes, would you give up when the initial sales are slow? You shouldn't because the premise hasn't changed. You are still a great baker. You just need to let more people know about your cakes.

What if you have invented a product and you don't know if there will be acceptance? Then you have to test the premise that your product is based on. For example, let's say you invented a luggage bag that also has gears and wheels that allow the user to ride it as a bicycle. You think people might buy this because airports are getting really large, and it takes a long time to get to the terminal or gate. So you think a luggage-bike might find many buyers who want to have an easier time moving around airports. But since no one in the world has ever seen such a product, it's hard to say if people will buy it. If you really did tap into an unmet need, you might sell a lot of it and make a lot of money. Conversely, it could turn out to be a dud because no one can get used to riding a luggage bag! What you need to do is make a few prototypes and give them to your friends to test your premise. If your friends don't like it and won't use it, it means your premise has failed, and there's no point persevering. You have to move on and invent something else.

When my venture started selling products online in the '90s, Internet adoption was still quite low. Most connections were still dial-up 56K, and broadband penetration was only 30 percent. Our premise was that broadband would become the standard and more people would go online to buy products. In the early years, the sales were very slow, and every time we were discouraged and felt like giving up, we would ask ourselves whether our premise had changed. And every time the answer was no because we believed that when broadband became more widespread, our sales would improve. So we decided to tough it out.

Of course, our premise proved to be true; when broadband became ubiquitous, our sales rocketed.

INTERNAL AND EXTERNAL MOTIVATIONS

The CEO who is running a transport business I invested in tells me he wanted to go into the bus transportation business when he was very young. After graduating from university, he joined a large transport company to learn the business. After that, he joined the government's Transport Ministry to understand things from the regulator's point of view. Thereafter, he joined the Transport Association to get to know all the bus company bosses in the country. *After that, he took a bus driving license to become a bus driver.* He bought a bus and started driving it. Once he understood how the business worked from a driver's point of view, he started working on the idea of a bus platform that he had.

When I ask him why it was so clear to him that he wanted to be in the bus business, he says, "I don't know why. From young, I've been fascinated with buses, and I just knew that this is what I wanted to do. I don't know what else I would do if I didn't do this."

That's what I like to hear when I invest in a company: that the entrepreneur has a very clear idea about who he is and what he wants. For this entrepreneur, being in the bus business was not just another business idea. He cannot see himself doing anything else. This is what I call having an internal motivation. This is very important when the going gets tough. For someone whose identity is very tied up with his work, he will not give up easily. He cannot think of doing anything else, so he will persevere and work hard to push through the tough times.

Contrast this to someone else who has a motivation simply to succeed. We saw a lot of such young people during the Internet craze. A lot of people thought that this was where the money was and wanted to make a lot of money. Making money is an external motivation. The desire is to succeed, and any idea will do. What happens when there is no instant luck and the going starts to get tough? These entrepreneurs will say, "This is too difficult. I have other ways to succeed that don't involve all this misery."

An external motivation is very shallow. People who chase success may find it elusive. People who are chasing their dreams are already living their success.

HOW TO CHANGE THE WORLD

Let's do a mental exercise. Let's say you step into a room with a happy person, and he is smiling and laughing and having a good time. You would be influenced and become happy also, right? Let's say on another day, you step into another room, but this one has a sad person who is crying. Would you also be sad? It's only human to be empathetic.

Now the question I have for you is this: What if the happy person steps into the room with the sad person? Will the happy person become sad, or will the sad person become happy?

Think about that for a while. What do you think? Got it? Well, the answer is this: *whoever is more insistent will influence the other.*

It is arguable that the good emotions have a natural advantage over the bad emotions. This is because human beings are able to function with only good emotions, and if we, as a race, were plagued by bad emotions all the time, we would not be able to survive. But the insistence principle still applies. If a sad person is absolutely insistent on being sad, he will spread sadness all around him. This flows nicely into a George Bernard Shaw quote:

> *The reasonable man adapts himself to the world: the unreasonable one persists in trying to adapt the world to himself. Therefore all progress depends on the unreasonable man.*

All progress depends on the unreasonable man who insists that the world adapts to him. People like Mahatma Gandhi and Martin Luther King Jr. were absolutely unreasonable people who refused to compromise and insisted that the world adapt to them. Few of us would be great men like Gandhi, but the principle is the same. If we have a belief about an idea, we have to put Positive Energy behind it until it works. We will see the world coming around to accept our ideas in time.

"I'VE BEEN HOLDING ON FOR A LONG TIME, AND STILL NOTHING"

Is the original premise still there? If yes, then are you giving it all the Positive Energy it needs? Do you have the right team in place?

If all yes, then you have to pull back and look at the very big picture. Is there a big industry change that is happening? For example, you could be the owner of a small grocery store and you are giving it all you got, but you are still getting fewer and fewer customers. You could be part of an industry trend where shoppers are going to large grocery chains like Walmart for greater variety and lower prices. You may believe that you provide the best service in the world for a grocery business, but you just can't fight against the scale of the big boys. I know something about the grocery business because I worked for P&G, and I can tell you that the scale of the big boys is massive. Their volume is so huge that they can get anything they ask for from suppliers like P&G. There is no way a small grocery shop can compete.

You have to try to do it differently. You cannot stay as you are and hope your luck will turn around. Can you choose a niche and do it better than the big companies? Can you find an alternative source of goods? Can you add a service? If you've tried all these things and nothing works, you have to think about packing it up before you lose more money. You will have the comfort in your mind that you have given it your all. But sometimes, some things happen in the world that work against you. There's no lack of disruptive trends. Automation, Internet, software, new inventions—these trends will make old things obsolete; there's just no way around it.

I had a friend whose father made precision screws for video and cassette tapes. If you are younger than thirty-five years old, you may be wondering what those things are. When the world began using fewer and fewer tapes, he just had to pack up his factory. The demand for tape screws simply disappeared.

WHAT JACK WELCH SAID

The examples I've given above have been about businesses and projects. What if you are in a job and you have been passed over for promotions a few times?

The first thing you do is to examine your performance. Talk to your boss and colleagues and find out from them how you can improve. Listen gratefully. They are giving you important feedback. If you look defensive when they are talking, they will simply shut up or tell you some unimportant stuff in order to not offend you. At the end, smile broadly and thank them for what they told you. And then work on the areas that you need to improve on.

Jack Welch, who was CEO at General Electric for over 30 years, has this to say about getting promoted:

The first answer is luck. All careers, no matter how scripted they appear, are shaped by some element of pure chance. Sometimes a person just happens to be in the right place at the right time...Sometimes we don't even know luck is good until well after the fact.

His advice for those who feel they have been passed over for promotions is this:

In the long run, luck plays a smaller role in your career than the factors that are within your control...Do deliver sensational performance, far beyond expectations, and at every opportunity expand your job beyond its official boundaries.

I have many friends who have chosen the treacherous path of climbing the corporate ladder and they agree wholeheartedly at this. Sometimes it's luck, but at the end of the day, it boils down to performance. When luck works against you, bide your time, be patient, and continue to perform. Do not lose your Positive Energy. Eventually, things will work out one way or another.

SCIENCE

One of the central pillars of positive psychology is to develop enduring character traits that will help us flourish in life. Patience, perseverance, and persistence are great qualities to have, but their "source" needs to be deep. If you do not believe deeply in what you are doing, you will find that trying to apply these qualities will exhaust you easily. If you do believe deeply, and you see that what you are persisting in defines who you are, you will push on despite great hardships.

CONCLUSION

I leave this chapter with a bit of poetry. We've all heard the line "All things come to those who wait." I wasn't sure where this line came from, so I checked. I discovered that it is part of a poem by Violet Fane

(1843–1905). Most people just quote the first line to make a point about patience. But the complete stanza goes like this:

> '*Ah, all things come to those who wait,*'
> *(I say these words to make me glad),*
> *But something answers soft and sad,*
> '*They come, but often come too late.*'

That last line changes everything! It's a lamentation that things often come "too late"! That means it is in this poet's experience that the "things" do come but later than what she had hoped or planned for. If you take this poem as a reflection of life, then don't give up too quickly! Plan to stay in the fight longer.

You want luck when you are ready. And it takes time for you to get ready.

LUCK FAVORS THE BRAVE

*All our dreams can come true, if we have
the courage to pursue them.*

—*Walt Disney*

I'M NOT GOING to give you a bunch of inspirational stories about how someone was brave enough to take a risk and how he succeeded. You can google for those.

Instead, I'm going to talk about what it really means to be brave.

IS IT COURAGE?

Imagine you and your friends are being pursued by serial killers. You arrive at a river, and there is a sign that says, "Danger: Alligators." One of your friends immediately grabs a rope, swims across the river, and pulls the rope taut so all of you can zip across to safety.

Now, is the friend that swam across the river brave? It depends.

What if afterward you ask that friend, "Hey, weren't you worried about the alligators?" and he replies, "Not really. The sign is a very old one. The alligators have all been rounded up and brought to the reserve. There are no alligators here."

Then you may think, "Oh, he's not really brave. He knew there were no alligators."

There're a few points to make with this story.

It's about having more information. As I've said in an earlier chapter, it's important to have more information. The more you know, the clearer you are about what risks exist. After you've done your research, you may discover that the risk is actually much lower than you previously thought. It's about taking calculated risks and knowing the odds, and jumping in when you have confidence that the odds are in your favor.

Only fools jump in without any information. They may get lucky and have nothing bad happen to them. They may even get very lucky and get some success. But if they keep jumping into rivers that have warning signs about alligators without first doing their research, it's a matter of time before they get eaten.

True courage is acting despite the information, and yet…Let's say your research tells you there are, in fact, many alligators, but you still decide to jump in to try to pull the rope across to save your friends. In this case, it is indeed true courage, where you take action despite knowing the odds are not in your favor.

And yet…do you really have a choice? In that kind of situation, wouldn't it simply make sense to "try your luck" and be brave? The alternative would have been just as bad. So there is another point to consider: *What is your alternative?* If your alternative is just as bad, you just have to take the risk.

COURAGE IN REAL LIFE

We are often faced with life-and-death decisions. It's just that because the threat is not immediate, we have the choice of postponing the decision. Even in the story I painted above, most people will not swim across the river to try to escape. They would prefer to take their chances with their pursuers, even if they know for a fact their pursuers will bring them harm. That's because the harm is delayed, so there's always a glimmer of hope versus the more immediate danger of being eaten by an alligator.

So many of us would rather be stuck in dead-end jobs, relationships, committees, and other commitments that we know are slowly sucking the life out of us than do anything about it.

I'm saying, just make that little bit of effort to research and find out more about what you can do and would like to do. You might find the risks are lower than you think and the rewards possibly greater.

WHAT IS YOUR DOWNSIDE?

In the story above, the downside is that you get eaten, so you're clear about the downside. But a lot of the things we encounter in our lives may seem like they have severe downsides when they actually don't. For example, you want to ask someone out on a date. What's the upside in that? She agrees to go out with you. What's the downside? *You pretty much go back to the situation you are in right now.* Here, the downside is psychological. In your mind you may feel like you are less of a person if you have been rejected. It might give you lower self-esteem so that you are afraid to ask anyone else out ever again. So that seems like a real risk.

But here again, the risk seems high because there is a lack of information. You could talk to her friends and ask if the odds of her saying yes to a date with you are high. Friends usually know. You could "lower the ask" (see the chapter titled "Attacking Good Luck") and not ask her on a date but just to do a class project together, to see if she would be willing to work on anything with you. If she says yes, her willingness to say yes to a date might not be so far away, particularly if you guys work well together on the project.

There's also the information about dates in general. What if your good friend told you he had been rejected by sixteen different people before he met his significant other? You might change your perception and think of dating as a "numbers game," that the more people you ask, the better your odds are.

But your friend's experience might also be a story of how the sting of rejection diminishes the more noes you get. If your friend tells you the early noes gave him *more confidence* (instead of less) to ask the girl he really likes out, then the *early rejection is simply training for greater courage* when the right one comes along.

RICH HABITS

I've quoted from Thomas C. Corley in an earlier chapter. He did a five year interview with 233 millionaires and authored the book *Change Your Habits, Change Your Life*. Here he is talking about courage and luck in an article for the *BusinessInsider* website on 13 February 2016:

> *Luck hides behind courage. Creating luck requires that you take risks. Taking risk requires courage. Courage is not the absence of fear, but the pursuit of something while in the throes of it. Overcoming fear is something you must cultivate as a habit.*

WHY DOES LUCK FAVOR THE BOLD?

It's mathematical. The more you try, the more chances you get, the greater your odds.

It's psychological. The more you try and fail, the more your mind toughens for the next try.

It's experience. You will be so much more experienced with more tries. You will know better what works and what doesn't.

So it's no wonder the person who tries a lot eventually gets a lucky break.

SCIENCE

Why do humans need to be brave? I think it comes from evolution. If our early ancestors had not taken that first step out of their comfort zone, we would not have evolved. They did it and were rewarded for it, which caused them to do it some more. Over time, humans discovered that it is important, at least for some members of the race, to venture out into the unknown and bring back information and rewards so all our lives can be improved. That's how we learned to admire those who have courage, and we have an innate desire to share our resources with them to help them in their goals.

In the end, all that's left is to be brave and try.

PART IV

EXPLAINING COMMON LUCK BELIEFS: FROM SUPERSTITION TO SCIENCE

LUCKY CHARMS AND JINXES

Man often becomes what he believes himself to be.

—*Mahatma Gandhi*

I have a friend who is a big Manchester United Football Club (MUFC) fan, but he doesn't watch any of the big games. He says that every time he watches a big game, MUFC will lose. Another friend of mine says he is actually a powerful wizard who can make the sky rain. He just has to wash his car, and it will rain within hours.

Another friend's superpower is even more awesome. He can move the entire stock market! He says all he has to do is start buying stocks and the stock prices will crash, or he will sell the stocks he has and the stock market will go up!

All of us have had these experiences, and maybe we develop certain beliefs over time. We believe we jinx the outcome of something simply because we are involved. We also believe that if we say something positive about something that hasn't happened yet, we will jinx it, and terrible things will happen.

On the opposite end of jinxes are lucky charms. These are supposed to bring good luck. Well-known examples include rabbits' feet, four-leaf clovers, and horseshoes. Some people think the things they wear—such as jewelry, watches, or even underwear—can be lucky. Some cultures believe that certain insects like the ladybird or animals like the turtle can bring luck.

LUCKY NUMBERS

Many cultures believe certain numbers bring good or bad luck. For the Chinese, it's easy to understand. The lucky numbers are those that sound like good words, and the unlucky numbers are those that sound like bad words. For example, the number 8 is considered lucky because it sounds like the word for "fortune" or "getting rich." There's an entire series of numbers that end with 8 that are considered lucky. So the obvious ones would be 88; 888; 8,888; and so forth. But 128 is also considered lucky because it sounds like the phrase "It's easy to get rich," and 168 is also well-liked because it sounds like the phrase "getting rich all the way." The series that follows from these could be 1,288; 1,688; 1,888; 2,888; and so forth.

The number 9 sounds like the word "a long time," so sometimes it is also combined with other lucky numbers to form a lucky series, such as 9,988. The number 3 is also considered lucky because it sounds like the word "life" in several Chinese dialects. So 13 is a lucky number because it sounds like "sure to live" in Cantonese. And 138 sounds like "a life of riches." The number 6 is particularly endearing to the Chinese who speak the Minnan dialect and who also speak English. It's pronounced "luck" in Minnan.

The unlucky number in Chinese is 4 because it sounds like the word "death." Some buildings in Hong Kong and China do not have a fourth floor or fourteenth floor because tenants or homebuyers will not want to rent offices or buy homes on those floors.

In the English-speaking world, thirteen is usually considered an unlucky number. There are several reasons for this. It has to do with events in history and in Christianity where the number thirteen preceded some bad events. For example, there were thirteen people at the Last Supper, and the thirteenth person, Judas Iscariot, ended up betraying Jesus. Also, the mass execution of the Knights Templar was thought to have occurred on Friday, October 13, 1307. A witches coven consists of thirteen witches, and when they come together, bad things happen.

Some buildings in the English-speaking world do not have a thirteenth floor, again, because tenants and homebuyers would avoid it.

The number seven is usually thought to be a lucky number. The nice things usually come in sevens, such as seven days in a week, seven main notes in the musical scale, and seven colors in the rainbow. The Christian God created the universe in six days and rested on the seventh day, so the seventh day is now a day of rest. Seven as a lucky and religious number is also used by the Indians, the Jewish and the Muslims.

Casinos in the West use the love for the number seven and have "Lucky 7s" in many of their games.

LUCKY ACTIONS

When I visited a historical palace called the Alcazar in Seville Spain, our guide pointed to a tiny carving of a doll's face on the walls and said that the architect had hidden nine such faces in the room, and legend has it that whoever found all nine faces would have tremendous luck. We only found four and we had to go.

All over the world, you would encounter things that you can do that the local people say would bring luck. Tossing coins into a water fountain or well is a well-known example. Touching the feet of statues is practiced in some cultures.

In Japan, I wrote my wishes on a piece of wood and gave it to a Shinto priest who uttered a prayer and then burnt hundreds of similar pieces of wood in a huge fire. In a small town in Malaysia, I touched the body of a humongous arowana as it swam by. In China, I tossed a coin into a giant intricately carved bronze urn and the guide said that I would only get good luck if the coin stood on its edge. Needless to say, visitors tossed a large quantity of coins to try and achieve that feat.

Whenever I am in these places, I would participate in these lucky activities because they are fun. But should I really believe that they will bring good luck?

How should we think about these lucky actions, jinxes, lucky charms, and lucky numbers?

EXPLANATIONS

The explanations in this chapter are going to be longer than the others in this part of the book because a few of the same effects can be observed across all the topics here.

EXPOSURE EFFECT

In the 1960s, psychologist Robert Zajonc showed that the mere repeated exposure of an object to a person would cause the person to first become familiar with it and, over time, to become fond of it. His research has been extended to people. The more you see someone, the more you will grow to like the person.

This explains why we love our friends. Even when we meet someone new who appears to be nicer than some of our friends (who, of course, can be a real pain in the butt sometimes), our feelings of happiness are not as high with the new person simply because we are not as familiar with them.

My first job was with Procter & Gamble, and a lot of the advertisements we did then were terribly uncreative but highly effective. You would remember them very easily. For Pampers, we compared it with Brand X, and we poured colored liquids into them to show that Pampers absorbed more liquid than Brand X.

For Head & Shoulders, we showed one side of the head washed with Head & Shoulders and the other side washed with Brand X. The side with Head & Shoulders would show no dandruff after two weeks, and the side washed with Brand X would still have dandruff.

Why do consumers remember these ads? It's simple. P&G brand managers had to ensure they outspent the competition in terms of advertising dollars. Our "share of voice," which was what we called it, always had to be higher. Basically, we'd expose the brand and the advertisement more often to the consumer than competitive brands. It's using the exposure effect at work.

There are some very famous stories in the field of architecture. For example, when the Eiffel Tower was first put up in Paris, the people hated it. Three hundred experts in design—among them prominent architects, artists, and sculptors—sent a petition called "Artists against the Eiffel Tower" to the minister of works to protest against it. But after it was built and people got to see it, they became used to it. Over time, they grew to be very fond of it.

It was the same with the Gherkin in London or the Esplanade Theatres in Singapore.

The exposure effect can be used to explain lucky numbers. Take seven for example. As I mentioned earlier, we see it in so many places. The number of days in the week, particularly, is a constant reminder. In a casino, the "Lucky 7" is promoted as lucky because people see it more than the other numbers. For example, in any dice game involving two dice, the sum of the two dice adding up to seven is higher than for any other number.

The number twelve also appears very often in our lives. We divide the day into twelve-hour halves, so we constantly see the number twelve on our clocks and watches. There are also many ways to arrive at twelve. It is divisible by one, two, three, four, and itself. The number thirteen, however, is a prime number that is divisible only by one and itself. You can imagine how merchants must have hated the number thirteen. There is no efficient way to pack thirteen items! Twelve can be nicely packed into a rectangular box 3 x 4, and we prefer rectangular boxes over square ones because they are easier to carry.

The primary reason the Chinese love the number eight is because it sounds like the word "to get rich." And it's everywhere in China. Even if you are a foreigner in China and you don't initially feel for the number eight, you are going to be bombarded by it so much that you will come to have feelings for it! This will be obvious when you go back to your own country. You are going to see the number eight appear in the most innocent places and feel good about it!

That's the exposure effect in action.

CONDITIONING

You've probably heard of Pavlov's dog. If not, here's a quick summary. Ivan Pavlov was a Russian scientist who discovered that his dog would salivate when it saw things it associated with food. Initially, Pavlov's lab assistant brought the food to the dog. Pavlov saw that the mere appearance of the assistant would make the dog salivate. It didn't matter whether the assistant was bringing food or not.

Pavlov took his experiment to the next level when he paired the appearance of food with a bell. After doing this a few times, the dog learned to associate the bell with the appearance of food and would begin to salivate at the ring of the bell even before any food was in sight.

He called this a conditioned response.

A lot of lucky charms are conditioned responses that came about as a result of coincidences. The friend who thinks he causes rain by washing his car has experienced several instances of it happening. And the friend who thinks the stock market conspires to reverse direction the moment he buys or sells has also experienced many incidences of that happening. These friends have developed conditioned responses of fear to the actions they performed because of the bad experiences.

It is the same with those who have rabbits' feet or lucky underwear. There is likely to have been a few positive outcomes associated with these lucky charms that led the owners to have conditioned responses to them. They feel lucky when they wear these things because of the lucky coincidences that have happened.

In terms of the numbers, the Chinese associate the number eight with so many positive things that it is not hard to develop a happy conditioned response to it.

Going back to Pavlov and the use of a bell, we also have a conditioned response to the sound of a particular type of bell—the one the ice cream truck rings! For me, whenever I hear the bell, I don't salivate with the thought of ice cream, but I do get good, happy feelings. This is because I've paired the sound of the ice cream bell to childhood memories of my parents buying me ice cream whenever the truck came around.

This was further reinforced when it was my turn to buy ice cream for my own kids. Whenever I hear the ice cream bell, the conditioned response is that I think about the times when I bought ice cream for my children, and I feel good.

CONFIRMATION BIAS

There is a tendency for human beings to seek out confirmation of our own beliefs as well as to recall memories in our minds in a way that supports these beliefs.

I have already described the power of beliefs in an earlier chapter. It is the same principle when applied to lucky charms and jinxes. If we believe they are real, we will see their effects everywhere.

When we say a person has a "confirmation bias", we mean that a person views and interprets events in a certain way that fits his beliefs rather than assess events objectively.

ATTRIBUTION

This is a very big area in psychology, and it's important to understand its impact on our minds.

Our reality is influenced by our perceptions. *Something has meaning to us because we assigned or attributed meaning to it. Different people who assign different meanings or explanations to the same phenomenon will arrive at different beliefs and understanding of the world.*

We can attribute meaning externally or internally. For example, if we slipped and fell on the pavement, we could attribute the accident to external reasons, such as the rain the previous night, a worn-out pair of shoes, or the incompetent contractor who was hired by the incompetent government. We could also attribute it to internal reasons, such as "Oh, I'm so clumsy," or "I have to be careful in my old age." Whether we attribute internally or externally more frequently can have an important impact on our psychology.

There is also a big difference in how people attribute events across different cultures. For example, the people in the West are generally more individualistic and absolute, whereas those in the East are more collectivistic or contextual.

When you take an event such as a parent beating a child, a Westerner's response might be to say, "The parent is so mean!" whereas an Easterner's response might be to ask, "Did the child do something wrong?" Here you see that a Westerner attributes being mean to the parent, because in a more absolutist culture, the act of beating a child is simply wrong.

In a more contextual culture, the question "Did the child do something wrong?" is natural because the contextualists accept that there could be situations where beating the child is the right thing to do. Also, raised in a culture of filial piety and respect for the elderly, the bias is toward the child being wrong, rather than the parent being mean. So our culture, which means the historical, religious, socioeconomic, political, and linguistic environments we grow up in, has an important impact on how we see and explain life.

One of my favorite examples is that of alien abduction. It seems aliens abduct only Americans! There are no reports of alien abduction anywhere else in the world. In other cultures, the feeling of being "experimented on" or "pressed upon" during sleep, coupled with temporary paralysis of the body, is attributed to the work of ghouls or demons.

Sleep studies by scientists over the last two decades offer a more mundane explanation. They call it sleep paralysis, and it is a condition that can happen to healthy adults and children during periods of abnormal sleep patterns or stress. The body cannot move during these moments of very active REM sleep, and it is often accompanied by hallucination and an acute sense of danger. These hallucinations and feelings of dread can seem very real, and lacking a scientific explanation, people looked for cultural clues to attribute the phenomena to. If you live in Midwest America, it is alien abduction. If you live in rural China, it is demon action. But if you live in the labs of sleep scientists, it's sleep paralysis. *You can see that what you call it makes a huge difference in how you see the world and how you continue to live your life afterward.*

SCIENCE

With the lucky charms, what happens is that constant exposure, conditioned associations, and misattributions cause a person to imbue a physical object with the power to bring about positive outcomes. Thereafter, through the confirmation bias effect, he or she starts to see the evidence of the lucky charm being effective in various avenues and explains away any evidence that might prove the lucky charm ineffective.

With jinxes, it's the same mechanics at work. It's just that the action or item has been paired with a negative outcome. Through the confirmation bias effect, the believer of the jinx starts to see the evidence of the bad effects everywhere, and this reinforces his or her belief in the jinx.

That's why so many people believe in lucky charms and jinxes.

CONCLUSION

At the core of it, lucky charms are just objects we hope will give us greater power to achieve what we want when we are feeling vulnerable and low. *So my sense is, if a physical object can do that, why not?*

I know a friend who wears a pendant from someone close to her who has passed to give her a sense of security and of being "watched over." Another acquaintance has a lucky pen he used to sign his first few deals, and he tucks the pen into his jacket every time he makes a major sales presentation to give him greater confidence. A relative of mine recently showed off a ring that has been passed down for many generations in her family, and she said the ring brings peace and harmony to the family.

It's great that these objects can do these things. It is not that we believe the objects themselves have the power. It is what the objects are able to trigger in us—feelings of security, confidence, peace, and other positive emotions—that gives us the power to cope with life's challenges and become more effective. Over a lifetime, if we can accumulate many of these objects, we will look at them fondly when we are old and consider ourselves lucky.

In front of my desk at home, I have the trophies I won from chess tournaments I participated in when I was young to remind myself that I can win. I have a gold-plated bull statuette to remind me of my ability to make money from the stock market. I have the medals I won from a series of sales competitions when I worked at Procter & Gamble to remind me that I can be a great salesman. Of course, I have pictures of my family, particularly of my kids when they were babies and toddlers. These are my lucky charms, and they give me the energy to press on with whatever I am working on. They are especially important when I am stuck or when I am feeling down. They remind me that I have the ability to figure things out. More importantly, they remind me of why I have to persevere.

Jinxes are just unfortunate coincidences, so we should keep telling ourselves they are not real and put them out of our minds.

But lucky charms and lucky numbers give us good feelings when we need them, so there's no harm in having them around us.

Lucky charms and lucky numbers are great!
Three thumbs up!

FENG SHUI

One touch of nature makes the whole world kin.

—*William Shakespeare*

If you've spent time in Asia, you will have encountered the concept of feng shui. It is also gaining popularity in the Western world. Feng shui is the ancient Chinese art of harmonizing the things in our life with nature and our environment. It is supposedly as ancient as Chinese civilization itself, about five thousand years old. The Chinese believe that if we harmonize our surroundings with the invisible forces called *qi* that bind the earth, the universe, and humanity together, we will have good luck. Many offices and homes in Asia are renovated after consultation with a feng shui master, who will advise the placement of certain things to maximize *qi* and bring good luck to all the occupants.

I have personally experienced interactions with feng shui masters many times. When I was in my twenties, I worked for a company that supplied office workstations and equipment. We were told by many feng shui masters to adjust our furniture this way or that to maximize luck. Typically, their advice consisted of adding natural elements like plants, water features such as fish tanks or fountains, and extra lights. There are also positions within every office that are "lucky" or "unlucky," so we had to move certain workstations around.

The practice of feng shui is closely tied to Chinese metaphysics and the Chinese religion of Taoism, so the explanations are almost always couched in metaphysical terms. That could be the main reason why many people are skeptical of feng shui, particularly people who are followers of other religions.

Is feng shui science or hocus-pocus?

ENVIRONMENTAL PSYCHOLOGY

When I studied psychology at the university, I came across a field of study called architectural psychology or environmental psychology. The study focuses on how human beings are affected by their surroundings. For example, negative effects are noise and air pollution, crowding, glaring lights, noxious smells, and jarring colors. Positive environmental effects could be secure personal spaces, quietness and solitude when needed, soothing music, natural lighting, and the presence of natural elements like water and trees.

When I look at these two subjects—feng shui and environmental psychology—I see that much of the advice in feng shui actually has a sound psychological base! The problem is that feng shui masters use metaphysical terms to explain the practices rather than scientific ones. For example, I once had a feng shui master tell me we needed to add more lights to a passage that led down a narrow staircase. He said, "This is a gateway to hell. We need to add lights to dispel the demons." Of course, we added the lights. It's not that we believed we would dispel any demons, but since we paid for the feng shui master, we thought we might as well use his advice.

After the lights were added, the workers in the office reported feeling more comfortable going down the narrow staircase. Now, if you explain this using feng shui terms, you might say that the demons have been dispelled. But using environmental psychology, you would simply say that human beings have a natural aversion to dark places, so well-lit spaces make us feel better!

Another example is when another feng shui master moved one of the bosses' tables from underneath a beam to a wider space that had a high ceiling. That boss reported feeling better and more productive.

Again the feng shui master explained it using feng shui metaphysics, but it has been proven in environmental psychology experiments that high ceilings reduce stress and the sense of crowding.

In yet another example in my experience, a feng shui master used a feng shui ruler to measure the height of the cashier machine in a retail shop. The ruler indicated that the cashier machine was placed at a height that was bad luck. The feng shui master recommended a change in height, or else luck and money would not flow into the machine. So we had to alter the entire counter to lower the height of the machine. As it turned out, the staff was very happy with the new height because it made using the machine easier. The Western-trained interior designer had used Western standards to determine the height of the counter. But Asians are generally smaller in build, and lowering the height made the cashier machine more comfortable for the staff (who were all Asians) to use. So here, feng shui metaphysics could be explained in the modern-day language of ergonomics, which is the study of people's efficiency in the work place, and a part of environmental psychology.

This is another example, published in a scientific journal: The psychologists at the University of British Columbia were interested in the effects of the color of interior walls. They recruited six hundred undergraduates and got them to perform a series of tests against red, blue, or neutral-colored backgrounds.

As it turned out, the students performed differently in different-colored rooms. The students who took the tests in the red condition were better at skills that required accuracy and attention to detail, such as spotting spelling mistakes. The scientists explained that this could be because red is associated with danger, which makes people more alert and aware. Students in the blue condition performed worse on short-term memory tasks, but did better on those requiring imagination, such as using geometric shapes to design a children's toy. The scientists explained that this could be because the color blue is associated with the sky and ocean, which puts the students in a relaxed mood to daydream.

SCIENCE

So I'm thinking (and I'm sure I'm not the only one) that feng shui is the ancient art of environmental psychology. It's just that in the past, there was no scientific process or language to describe the discovery that humans respond differently to different environmental factors. So gods and demons and invisible forces were created to explain the phenomenon. It's what I said in the introduction to this book: Gods and demons were used in the past to account for things we didn't understand. But when we developed a proper understanding of things, we had no more need for them.

So we can create the art of modern feng shui, where it's about creating the spaces around us that set us in the best moods and enable us to perform optimally. And we can explain the reasons for why we should design our spaces that way based on sound psychological and physical reasons and not use metaphysical ones. Here are some suggestions I personally use to better my mood and increase my effectiveness.

Ergonomics: In an earlier chapter, I described the state of "flow," or being in "the zone" where you can work for hours. This can happen only if your workstation is set up in an ergonomic manner. If not, you will feel stresses and aches in your shoulders, neck, or back, which will stop your flow soon enough.

It is massively important to get the right chair that gives you the best back support because you are likely to be sitting in it for hours on end. I prefer a chair that is made from netting, such as the Herman Miller Aeron chair, because I feel it promotes air circulation. If you are from a colder climate, you might prefer a leather chair. The chair must be lowered to a level where you can put your feet firmly on the ground. If not, you need to put a stool or leg stand underneath your table so you can place your feet on it. Or else, you will feel your legs getting tired very fast, which will place stresses on your legs and back.

Your computer monitor should be at your eye level with your head held upright. If it is lower or higher, you will develop stresses in your neck and shoulders. This means that it is a terrible idea to use a laptop because you will be looking down all the time. If you are using a laptop, you should either connect a separate monitor to it and prop it up to eye level, or you can connect a separate keyboard and then prop up the laptop's screen to your eye level.

Work environment: Ideally, your workstation should give you exposure to natural elements like sunlight, trees, plants, water, and wood. It is also important that air circulates well. Feng shui has many explanations for how each one of these elements creates *qi* to make us feel better and bring us luck. But the scientific explanations are just as plenty and more believable.

For example, negative ions are created by the presence of running water, and they clear the air of airborne allergens such as pollen, mold spores, bacteria, and viruses. Oxygen is given out by plants, which nourishes our minds and helps us think better, and sunlight creates the hormone called serotonin in our bodies, which makes us happy. These are all invisible effects the ancient Chinese might have called *qi,* but we call them by more scientific names.

We can trace the scientific evidence for every element of nature, but here is the simple version: *humans have always enjoyed interacting with nature.* So having elements of nature in your workstation will elevate your mood and make you more productive.

Colors: We've read that colors can affect our moods and performance. So the best thing to do is to have neutral and earthy colors in your workstation or office, or a mix of colors so that no single color overwhelms your workspace. You don't want to be sitting in a blue room when you have to perform tasks that need urgent attention to detail. You also do not want to sit in a red room when you need to come up with imaginative solutions.

Security: This was a major concern of our ancestors when they lived out in the open or in caves. They needed to be able to defend themselves if threats came at them. In the office environment now, I can detect three types of security-related arrangements that are optimal to performance.

One is to face the main door. You'd want to face the door that people are coming in and going out of. If your back is to that door, you will feel unsafe, distracted, and constantly on edge. You will not be able to have the peace of mind to focus on your work. The second is having your back to the wall. This was how our ancestors in the cave preferred it. With a wall at their back, they could be confident that no enemies or wild animals would come from the back. The third is personal space. The rage now in office arrangements is "open plan," where everybody's computer screen and workstation can be seen. On the one hand, it may seem like this forces everyone to concentrate on their work and not to skive, since skiving can be seen by the boss, but on the other hand, emerging research shows that such public spaces do not let employees feel secure, and do not give them the peace they need to contemplate creative ideas.

CONCLUSION

The old feng shui masters say feng shui can bring us luck. But I think it is just that *properly planned environments can create optimal conditions for us to perform at our very best.* When we are performing at our very best, we create the conditions for good things to happen to us. If your office is thinking of engaging a feng shui master to help plan your office, my view is that there is no harm in doing so. Think of all the advice as likely to have sound scientific bases, even if the master himself does not use the language of science.

Just be careful about advice that is clearly religious and superstitious in nature that does not have any foundation in science. For example, I once had a feng shui master who said we had to install a statue of the Taoist god of the earth in a particular location because it was facing the main door. There is no way we can find a scientific basis for that advice. And having a god from a particular religion installed in the office would be insensitive to the believers of other religions. So it's best to discard that kind of advice.

I think in time the practice of feng shui will be gradually replaced by environmental psychologists, who will have evidence-backed advice for us to plan our living and work spaces so we can maximize our ability to perform. We can then have confidence that having the right environment will enhance our abilities and thereby increase our chances of good luck!

Feng shui is environmental enhancement for peak performance!
Four thumbs up!

KARMA

*I'm a true believer in karma. You get what
you give, whether it's bad or good.*

—SANDRA BULLOCK

"KARMA" IS A Sanskrit word that has complex meanings in Buddhism and Hinduism, but broadly it's about what you reap and sow. Everything you do is a cause that produces effects, which are, in turn, causes for other effects that can ripple through reality.

A central belief of Buddhism is that karma keeps score, and if you do good things, you can expect to receive good returns. If you do bad things, you will receive bad returns. Sometimes the returns come in this life, but sometimes they come in your next life. The Hindus and Buddhists believe in reincarnation, and if you've done a lot of bad things, your next life may be filled with difficulties, or you may even reincarnate into a lower form of life, such as an animal or insect.

Good and kind deeds produce good returns in this life and the next. It is the central tenet of Buddhism that the enlightened person has good thoughts, speech, and action and creates good karma for himself. The good karmic returns elevate the individual from one life to another until he eventually achieves enlightenment and is free from the sufferings of this world.

But karma cannot be forced. You cannot do good *expecting* to get rewards in return. If you do, it makes the good things you do a part of your calculative, manipulative, and greedy mind-set, which will create

146

bad karma. You have to do good *without* the expectation of return. If you can do that, you will create good karma for yourself, and good things will eventually find a way to you.

I googled for quotes on karma and found this one that I thought was quite smart:

Whatever it is life gives to you, remember, you started it.

The principle of karma—that you reap what you sow—is an easy-to-understand rule for creating good luck. First, do good and become the good luck for others, and then good luck will come back to you.

SOCIAL EXCHANGE THEORY

Psychologists and sociologists have written about social exchange from the late 1950s onward. It describes human interaction in economic terms, where every individual has a cost-benefit analysis to the relationships he or she maintains with others. If the costs and benefits are assessed to be fair by both parties in a relationship, the relationship will continue. If one side feels he or she is giving more than the other side, the relationship will eventually end. For example, let's say a colleague of yours starts to give you a ride to work every day. From your point of view, you save on transport and get a free daily ride to work, which is great. From your colleague's point of view, however, the cost-benefit analysis will not be in his favor. He will have to incur extra gas costs because of the extra weight his car has to carry, and he will be increasing the wear and tear on his car. He also has to expend extra effort to coordinate with you on the ride.

If this is a short-term arrangement, it's not a problem because the basis of any relationship is that you can do small favors for each other without needing a return. But if this becomes a long-term arrangement, social exchange theory predicts that conflict will arise, and the relationship will eventually break down because of the cost-benefit imbalance. To resolve the conflict, you have to balance the economic exchange. If you propose to pay your colleague a price that covers his gas, the wear and tear, and the extra effort, the cost and benefit would square up, and he should be happy to continue the car-riding relationship with you.

Other psychologists have written that indirect or intangible benefits can be used in a social exchange. In the car-riding example, instead of getting money from you, your friend might be happy to get privileged information from you or get your help with an important contact he needs. There could also be psychological benefits. Let's say you are a sports celebrity in your town. Your colleague might be happy to give you a free ride to work every day because he enjoys the ego boost from being seen with you. That psychological benefit can square off the exchange and keep the car-riding relationship stable.

Now, let's understand the theory from the other side of the exchange. Let's say your colleague gives you the free ride to work, and in his mind, he has already worked out that the exchange is fair; let's say it's because he feels he is getting privileged information at work that helps him with his job.

But you might not know this, and you start to feel that the exchange is unfair to your colleague because you keep getting free rides. You will try to square the exchange by offering payment, but your colleague might decline it because he doesn't want to be "overpaid." Social exchange theory predicts that your inability to square off the exchange may make you feel bad enough that you find alternative transport arrangements and terminate this relationship.

Put simply, social exchange theory is this: if someone does something for you, you will want to do something that's equal in value in return. You can express it another way: if you do something for someone, he or she will want to do something of equal value for you.

HOW TO HARNESS IT

When I first bought my place in the late '90s, I had a carpenter who did up all the cabinetry in my house. He was a quiet man, but he did good work, so I was very happy with what he was able to deliver.

Two weeks after he fully handed over the project, he appeared at my home. I was surprised to see him because the project had been fully delivered, and all payment had been made. He said, "I was in the neighborhood, and I just wanted to check on the cabinets." I just thought that this was excellent service and let him in. He went about tightening the screws in the cabinets he had made for us and then left.

Another four months later, he came again to the house and said the same thing. He was in the neighborhood and just wanted to check on the cabinets. This time around, he pulled out a door and said that the laminate was not stuck on properly. He said he would take it back to the factory to have it fixed. Three days later, he brought back the door. Over the years, we kept seeing him on and off. He would be "in the neighborhood" and drop by. He did not attempt to become friends with me or talk to me about anything else. He simply went about checking his cabinets and then fixed little things here and there. And he never charged me for any of it.

I ended up recommending over twenty friends to him. Those friends of mine also said they had recommended their friends.

What happened?

I can see four effects. One is the exposure effect, which I have explained in the chapter "Lucky Charms." We saw him so often that we grew to like him and trust him. The other effect is the social exchange effect. He made us feel that he has done a lot for us, and we felt we needed to do something back.

If he hadn't appeared constantly, we might have forgotten about him. At least we would not be as active as we were in introducing our friends. But because he kept appearing, he kept us at the forefront of our minds, so this is the top-of-mind effect. What happens is that whenever we hear that a friend of ours is planning to renovate his or her home, we quickly recommend him because we have strongly paired the idea of renovations with him in our minds.

The fourth effect is the story effect. I tell my salespeople they must not only be good in their service; they must attempt to create stories that their clients can tell of them. This is how word of mouth can spread widely, when an interesting story can be told easily. This is how you become legendary in your field, when many stories are told of you. My carpenter did that with the constant and free touch-ups he did in my house. I liked it so much that I tell the story in my sales seminars, and I'm telling it here.

This is how he has become legendary. His excellent service and constant giving without expectation of return have rippled through a reality greater than himself. He is getting business now from someone who heard it from someone who heard it from me at a sales seminar and asked for his contact.

If you want a simple way to remember this, call it great sales karma.

BE APPRECIATIVE

Are you the kind of person who notices a great day? When the sun is up, the air is clear, and the temperature is just nice, do you say, "Wow, what a great day"? Or are you always too bogged down with your worries that you don't have time for such trivial things? I believe there are a lot of small blessings in life that the universe gives to us, like a nice day, a pleasant stranger who offers a happy smile, a word of encouragement from a friend when you most need it, a kiss from a loved one, a thank-you note from a customer or a senior, a beautiful rainbow, a giant tree or lovely plant; there's a lot of beauty and goodness that we can see if we open our eyes. Often we take these things for granted, or we don't even notice them because we are so distracted by other things.

Cultivating an appreciative mind-set would make us happier people. We are already receiving good karma all around, so we have to learn to enjoy its effects. That's the passive form of being appreciative. The active form of being appreciative is to be conscious of the good things being done for us and paying it back or forward with praise, a pat on the back, a huge smile, or a random act of kindness to a stranger.

Giving praises and encouragement is the easiest form of giving that creates good karma. It just takes a few words. It starts with noticing good work and good effort by the people around us. Then, we take a moment to enjoy that work and feel happy that we were able to witness it. And then we should remember to be verbally appreciative and tell the person what it is that we enjoyed. "Bob, that's a nice tie!" "Darling, thanks for the yummy dinner." "Hey, Mum, the kids are always refreshed after spending the afternoon here with you and Dad." "Boss, that presentation was impressive!"

Is it brown-nosing and sucking up? It is if you are not doing it willingly and happily but with a goal in mind. It's not if they are all honest appreciations of the good things you have in your life. The people around you may think you are a suck-up initially, but they will eventually know it's just the way you are, and you do it to everyone, and you do it all the time.

Is it a lot of effort to constantly notice these things and say them? It will be if you are not doing it willingly or naturally. You will feel like it is just one more thing you have to remember to do in a day and feel even more stressed than before. But it is not a burden if you first learn to enjoy the good things around you. Just learn to notice them and enjoy them without saying anything at first. After a while, you can just let the social exchange effect take over. When you feel you are at the receiving end of nice things, you will start to feel like you should reciprocate, and the easiest way is to say something nice to square off the exchange. At that time, in your own mind, the exchange is squared off, but in the minds of the people around you, it may not be. They may feel you are a person of tremendous positive and honest energy, and they may want to give back to you the Positive Energy you gave to them.

That's when good karma happens.

GIVER'S HIGH

Creating good karma is about giving without expecting return. But some people might feel exhausted if they feel like they keep giving and they get nothing back. If you feel this, you are not giving the right way.

You don't have to "give till it hurts." As mentioned above, you start by noticing the good things you are getting, and you will naturally want to give because you feel you have received a lot.

What is exhausting is actually the *expectation* that there should be something in return. If there is no expectation, it won't be exhausting. A trick to remove the expectation is to see that the exchange has already been squared off the moment you give. You give because you enjoy giving, and *the enjoyment in itself is the payment for your giving.* Research has shown that being generous lights up the pleasure centers in our brains. There is a phenomenon called helper's high, or giver's high, that causes the givers to experience improvements in mood and immunity.

So you are already deriving benefits from your acts of giving and helping. The fact that others are likely to give you something good in return is an added bonus.

SCIENCE

I would say that karma is social exchange theory plus the positive psychology that comes with giving.

All of us have heard people say, "I have a very simple philosophy in life. If people are good to me, I will be good to them. If they are bad to me, I will be bad to them too." You have heard people say that, haven't you? Well, right there is the secret to having everyone in the world be good to you! *You just have to be good to them first.* When you do, you create a positive balance in the exchange with others that will cause them to naturally be good to you to equalize the exchange.

CONCLUSION

The philosophy of karma says that it's *not* simply a one-to-one exchange. It is not "you give him, he gives you back," period. There are unseen effects and ripples of effects that you can cause with your good words and deeds. You praise someone and he might feel more confident and start something important that benefits other people. You help another and she might feel happier and perform a random act of kindness for someone else.

If you are the initiator of these good deeds, you will create a sphere of Positive Energy and positive people around you, and these will lead to greater possibilities of good luck happening to you.

Cultivate good karma for great luck!
Five thumbs up!

PRAYER

If you're going to believe in God, if you're going to
take that leap of faith, as I do, then the God that
seems the most comprehensible to me would be the
God who set us spinning and said 'Good luck.'

—R*OGER* R*OSENBLATT*

I AM NOT a member of any religion, but I think all religions are great.

When I travel to Europe, I visit amazing churches. In China and Japan, I go to these beautiful Buddhist, Taoist, Shinto, and Zen temples. In India and other places in Central Asia and Southeast Asia, I see intricately designed Hindu temples and majestic mosques. Everywhere I meet people who are deeply devoted to their religions and who are compassionate, serene, and wise.

I just want to make clear at the outset of this chapter that it is not my intention to discount the power of religion and the belief in God. I believe in God myself; it's just that I borrow from the wisdom of all the religions instead of subscribing to one. I just want to deal with this subject about prayer and luck. I do see that prayer works in helping bring about lucky events and opportunities. The immediate attribution, of course, is that the God whom the prayer is directed to has answered the prayer. I'm not saying it is untrue that God directly answers prayer because I have no way to show that, but I would like to offer some other explanations here.

MEDITATION

Deep prayer is a kind of meditative state, and there is a huge body of research that shows meditation has tremendous benefits.

<u>Physical benefits.</u> Meditation has been shown to help lower blood pressure. One particular study shows that high blood pressure patients who meditated could stop taking their blood pressure medication. Another study shows that meditation helps the brain regenerate brain cells. So people who meditate feel better physically.

<u>Mental benefits</u>. Meditation reduces stress and increases self-awareness and concentration. It increases the brain's ability to focus and process information. One study shows that people who learn to meditate can increase the gamma waves in the brain. Gamma waves are responsible for peak performance, concentration, inspiration, creativity, insight, clarity, flow, and those big aha moments.

<u>Social Benefits</u>. Meditation increases compassion and empathy. It increases feelings of connectedness and social well-being. It lowers worry and loneliness and reduces feelings of anger, frustration, and helplessness.

People who pray deeply tell me that when they are in prayer, they have an overall sense of well-being, a feeling of the presence of God or of being connected with the universe. The ironic thing is that they say it actually reduces the kinds of things they feel they want in their lives! *It is the people who pray shallowly who are concerned with wanting things.* Those who pray deeply have reached a higher level of spirituality, and they do not ask for things for themselves.

With all these benefits from the meditative qualities of prayer, it is easy to see that it can lead to increased performance and Positive Energy, which then attract lucky possibilities.

VERBALIZING YOUR THOUGHTS

I talk to myself. A lot.

I go for long walks as a part of my exercise regimen, and I talk to myself when I walk. And I don't just talk; you can see my hand gestures complementing what I'm saying. In an earlier time, I might have been locked up as a crazy person. But now, people just assume I am talking into a really tiny earpiece that's connected to a phone somewhere in my body!

It is very different when I think about something in my head and when I hear myself talk. When I talk, I realize I can clarify my thoughts better. I am better able to put my emotions into it, and then I see better the decisions I need to make. Even if you don't talk to yourself constantly, you might have experienced this too. You are talking to a friend about something, and as you verbalize your thoughts, you discover how you really feel about it, and it becomes clear what you should do next.

Studies are emerging to show that people who talk to themselves perform better at tasks that require memory recall and logical processing. Apparently, geniuses like Albert Einstein talk to themselves constantly. Celebrities like Jennifer Lawrence and Kanye West also claim to talk to themselves regularly.

So in my mind, this is another effect of prayer. I think as we verbalize our thoughts in prayer, what we need to do becomes clearer. The aha moment can come with a shot of gamma waves in the brain, so I imagine it can feel like there is a reply from God.

If you don't pray, try talking to yourself, or talk out loud. Or you can address the "person in the sky" if you are not part of any religion. You can stick on an earpiece, and you can talk as loud as you want, and people will leave you alone!

REPETITION

When we keep repeating something to ourselves, it focuses our minds and wills.

People pray in different ways. There are those who pray casually and ask for things almost as an afterthought, like "Oh, by the way, if it's not too much trouble, can you also help me win the lottery this weekend?" I think this kind of prayer wouldn't work because it's not very sincere! There is no way any God would take it seriously because the person who is praying is not even serious himself.

But the people who are sincere in their prayer and who ask for the same things over and over again have a different type of conversation with God. They don't just ask for something in a few words. They will talk about all the things that are going on with their lives, the different people their requests will affect, and what they will do if their requests are answered. *It's a detailed plan of action that just needs that one divine intervention, that one lucky break!*

I think as we keep repeating a goal to ourselves or to God, the vision of it happening becomes clearer and clearer, and we start to orientate our lives toward that goal, making it easier and easier for that possibility to happen.

THE WILL

In an earlier chapter, I talked about the finches Charles Darwin studied. Those that lived on islands with more cacti developed longer beaks in order to pick the seeds off the fruit of the cacti. Those that lived on islands where there were fewer cacti developed a taste for small bugs and lived closer to the ground. These developed short, tough beaks in order to catch and crush the insects. I also pointed out that modern-day scientists have even been able to isolate the genes responsible for the lengths of beaks in finches.

I'm thinking about the finches that were on the island with the cacti. The early finches did not have very long beaks, but they developed longer beaks over time. *How exactly did they develop these longer beaks?* Was it a decision they made? Like, did they analyze the situation, call for a meeting, and say, "Hey, guys, you know, we are on an island that has elongated flower petals, and in order to get at the seeds, we need longer beaks"?

No, *they basically just tried very hard to get at the seeds.* And in "trying very hard," they started to influence their genes in such a way that their offspring had longer beaks. Their offspring also tried very hard, and through successive generations of finches trying hard, the beaks of finches became longer and longer.

I call this "trying very hard" the will. And the will is a very powerful thing that can change our genes to help us adapt to our environment. I don't want to sound like I am writing a superhero novel, where there are people with special skills who can bend metal with their wills. But I think when we are completely focused on something and working hard at it and we are willing it to happen with our efforts and our prayers, it does happen.

There is no science experiment I can find that talks about the human will. So it is a logical leap that I am making by asking the question about the finches. It is the question of evolution. When we see evidence of different species of animals adapting to their environment, we have to ask, What was it that caused it?

We see evidence of evolution from different types of human beings too. The Inuit people who live in the Arctic have a gene that the rest of us who live near the equator don't and that helps them withstand the cold better. The Africans, of course, have evolved darker skins to help them withstand the sun.

Whenever human beings were faced with adverse circumstances, like extreme cold or sun, we basically had two choices: we could leave (which was not so easy to do in the early days), or we could decide to resist against the adverse conditions. When our early ancestors decided to resist, I say that they willed themselves into becoming more resistant and caused their DNA to change in a way that helped them survive and thrive.

So I see the human will, or, in fact, the will of all living things, to survive and thrive, to be powerful. And I think the will is expressed when we are in deep prayer. We have a power to manifest in ourselves the kinds of physical and mental resources we need to survive and thrive.

SCIENCE

Prayer is meditation, focus, and the concentration of mind and effort.

I think when someone prays and asks to win the lottery or otherwise gain some easy luck, the prayers will not be answered. There is no focusing of the mind and no concentration of will and effort.

But I think when someone prays and constantly asks for personal qualities like wisdom and strength, his or her mind is focused through repetition and the meditative quality of prayer. That person will start to achieve clarity of mind and purpose and acquire those personal qualities he or she asks for.

I just want to add a note here to nonbelievers of God that just because we can identify scientific explanations for why prayer works does not mean we have *proven* that God does not exist and does not answer prayers. It is logically wrong to make that jump. As yet, there are no scientific ways to prove or disprove God's existence, and that's why believers of God say that they have faith. I find that faith may be one of the most powerful of human motivators yet, and it gives strength and hope to many people who are going through tremendous hardships in life. I can't go too deeply into a discussion about God in this book; it's not what this book is about. I clearly don't believe in all the various gods of the little things our ancient ancestors believed in, but I don't find it illogical to believe that a greater power created the Big Bang and set everything in motion. I am not saying it is true or not true. I am saying it is *not illogical* to believe in God or not to believe in God.

CONCLUSION

I find the saying "God helps those who help themselves" to be reasonable. When prayer is a part of a good overall plan where a lot of Positive Energy is being directed toward that plan, the prayer will work because it aligns the person's spiritual self with everything else he or she is doing.

When I ask people what they want luck for, I find that many have difficulty verbalizing their thoughts and emotions. When that is the case, their vision for themselves cannot be clear, and they cannot focus their energies to achieve their goals. This is made worse if their daily lives are filled with stress.

So one of the things I say to them is to try to pray if they are, or have been a part of, a religion and know the practice and ritual of prayer. If they are not part of a religion, I say, "Try to talk to the 'guy in the sky.'"

Human beings have always looked up and talked to the heavens since we came about, so it is not such a strange thing to do. Some psychologists have shown that the simple act of lifting your head and looking up helps you access a different part of your brain and makes you feel better.

So lift up your heads, quieten your spirit, and just talk. You may find that the universe replies.

Deep prayer is powerful!
Five thumbs up!

👍👍👍👍👍

GAMBLING LUCK

---

*Victory is a fleeting thing in the gambling
business. Today's winners are tomorrow's
blinking toads, dumb beasts with no hope.*

—Hunter S. Thompson

You've heard some people say that they have good "gambling luck" and others say that they never have gambling luck. What is this thing called gambling luck?

There are many interesting psychological processes involved in gambling. The casinos especially have worked out devious ways to keep you coming back. This is what's at work for someone who gambles.

SELECTIVE SHARING AND NEWS

Why do we hear more stories of people winning at the casino than losing? Is it possible that some people have better luck than others at the casino?

People are more likely to share stories of winning at a casino because it is exciting. When they lose, they will keep quiet or say, "I won some and lost some," which is a way of saying they lost in the end. People think that losing at a casino is for losers; that's why they keep quiet. After all, don't James Bond and all the other successful men in the movies always win at the casino? This "selective sharing" is what accounts for stories of people winning at casinos.

Then there are the big wins where the casinos' public-relations departments go into hyperdrive. Whenever someone wins a big jackpot at the casino, the casino's PR team will make sure the whole world knows about it. They will position the winner as some common man on the street who simply got lucky. The subliminal message is that anyone can win at the casino, including you, so please come in and try your luck. Whenever there is news in the media about gambling, it's about somebody winning. So it seems like lots of people are winning.

But there is no mention about the tens of thousands of people who lose money every day.

CASINO ODDS

Forget all those spy movies that glamourize gambling and always show the leading man winning at the casino. In every game in the casino, there is a house advantage built into the games. Here is a simple summary.

1. In roulette, two green numbers, 0 and 00 give the house roughly a 5 percent advantage. What this means is that out of every 100 turns of the roulette table, the odds of the ball landing on a green number is actually 5 times. If you simplify it, it means once in every 20 turns.

2. In blackjack, the casino will take your money after you bust even before it looks at its own cards. This gives it roughly a 6 percent advantage.

3. For poker in a casino, the house takes a small cut out of every pot for providing the service of dealing the cards at the table and the facilities of the casino. This cut is a constant leakage that will ensure everyone loses in the end.

4. For jackpot, the odds are programmed into the computers that run the machines. Most machines pay small sums frequently to keep giving the players the thrill of winning. But in the long run, the machines will take in more than they give out. There is

a story that the machines that make a lot of noise when someone wins are usually placed at the entrances of casinos so people will keep hearing the winning sounds, think it is easy to win, and go into the casinos.

The odds vary for the other games, but by and large, casinos have a 3–7 percent advantage in the games. Casinos that operate in regulated regimes like Las Vegas have their games and machines audited by the authorities regularly to ensure they stay within the regulated limits of the odds they are allowed to set. These built-in advantages will ensure the house wins in the long run.

In the short run, you may have a winning streak that can be very exciting and give you the sense that the gods are smiling down at you. But as we learned in the chapter "Know the Odds and How to Bet," the law of large numbers will eventually set in, and the advantage the house has will always play out. There are no gods smiling at you or leaving you. It's just the odds playing out. The odds predict that you *will* win some, but you *will* lose more.

YOU *SHOULD* LEARN TO GAMBLE

Even though I say you will lose more than you win when you gamble, I don't mean that you should avoid it altogether. In fact, I encourage everyone, including my own children, to gamble a little bit all the time, in order to get a good sense of how odds work and to get used to betting money and taking risks. Since I believe life is more like a game of poker (or mah-jongg in the Chinese context), it is important to learn how poker or mah-jongg works.

When gambling with friends, the odds are the same for everyone since there is no house advantage, so the skills count. And the so-called skills in gambling are really about being able to run the numbers in your head and calculate the odds of each of your hands very quickly and make the right moves and bets. This makes you better at numbers and at assessing risk. I believe that this is a skill that translates well into real life.

You've heard the saying "Life is a gamble." It's about taking reasonable risks. But for many people, there is a certainty bias. They don't want to do anything unless there is certainty in it. My opinion is that having this certainty mind-set will not cause us to be very lucky in life.

The world is changing at a very rapid rate. Everyone is trying to eat your lunch. You may think you have a stable job, but it is hard to foresee the situation a few years down the road. Your company might restructure, your job might be replaced by a machine, or you might get a new boss who for some strange reason doesn't get along well with you. Learning to take some risks will keep you plugged in to the world because you need to know what is going on. It will also keep you nimble-footed and alert to opportunities and threats as they arise. It is going to take more to survive in the future than it did in the past.

So remove the idea that you can get rich from gambling. But gamble a little bit as a form of entertainment that also sharpens your sense of odds and risk-taking.

CAREER GAMBLERS

What about the professional poker or mah-jongg players who make a living from gambling? Don't they win all the time? No, they don't. The career gamblers don't just make money from gambling. They make money from exhibitions, training, and sponsorship deals. They are hired by the casinos to promote and glamourize gambling so more people will do it.

Some professionals got rich through other means (there are some Hollywood actors and some Internet millionaires who regularly compete on the poker circuit), and they have the money to ante up for the competitions. Otherwise, many players are sponsored by casinos and other corporate sponsors (such as gambling equipment makers) to play in the competitions.

Do not think that these professional gamblers make their living from winning in gambling all the time or become rich from gambling. It is a trap. That is the impression they want to create to lure you into gambling.

INTERMITTENT REINFORCEMENT

If people lose more than they win, why do people keep gambling? To understand this, you need to understand what an intermittent reinforcement schedule is.

There is a school of psychology called Behaviorism, which explains human behavior in terms of the reflexes we have to external stimuli such as rewards and punishment. The thinking is best explained through the early experiments with animals that the researchers in this field did.

Suppose you want to teach a bird to press a lever in its cage. You can make the lever brightly colored in order to attract its attention. When the bird is hungry, it will explore its surroundings for food and will likely press the lever. When it does that, a pellet of food drops into its cage, and it is able to eat. The bird then learns that pressing the lever gives it food. If every time the bird presses the lever it gets rewarded with food, the lever-pressing behavior of the bird will be consistent and predictable. It will press the lever only when it needs food. This is known as *direct positive reinforcement*.

What if you want to increase the lever-pressing behavior of the bird? You could change the food delivery to one food pellet with every five presses of the lever. There will be some confusion in the beginning when the food doesn't come on the first press of the lever. The bird will become frantic and press the lever a few more times. When the food comes out at the fifth press of the lever, the bird will learn that more presses of the lever are required for the food to come out. After a while, it will learn that it takes five presses of the lever to get the food. This is known as a *regular reinforcement schedule*.

What if you want to increase the lever-pressing behavior even more? You can make the reinforcement schedule *intermittent*. This means that sometimes the food comes once in a few lever presses, and sometimes it comes after many lever presses. The bird knows it needs to press the lever to get food, but *it is uncertain about how many presses are needed for the food to come out*, so it keeps on pressing until it gets the amount of food it wants.

When you apply this to gambling, you'll have a better insight into why people keep gambling or even become addicted to it. The "lever-pressing behavior" is the gambling. The "food" reward is comprised of an emotional and a financial reward. The financial reward is known because it depends on how much the gambler bets, but it is the emotional high that is the bigger reward.

Human beings love to win, and we are able to endure all kinds of hardships in order to win. When our early ancestors were hunters, they learned that it takes a long time and a lot of effort to be rewarded with the fruits of the hunt. When they were farmers, they learned that they had to till the fields for many months before it was time to harvest. So we learned to suppress and endure long hardships so we can enjoy the fruits of the work when they come. And when they do come, we celebrate in a big way and revel in the satisfaction of a reward that is well-earned.

This is played out on the gambling table. The gambler is looking for that win, and he loses track of the money he is losing. The pain of the losses is endured and suppressed in the subconscious mind in the process of looking for the win. With the randomness of gambling, the wins come in an intermittent way, causing the gambler to "keep pressing the lever" to look for that emotional high.

OTHER INTERMITTENT REINFORCEMENT SCHEDULES SITUATIONS

Since I am on the subject, I will just touch a little bit on the other situations in life where we find intermittent reinforcement.

Being in an abusive relationship is one. If you have ever wondered why people stay with their abusive significant others, it's because the moments of strife are seen as the "hard work" they have to put into a relationship. The moments of intimacy are the rewards for the hard work, and they are made more intense by the earlier abuse. And because the moments of intimacy are intermittent—the abused person doesn't know when his or her significant other will be nice—the emotional highs are even more powerful than normal.

I've seen bosses do this with their subordinates. They might not know they are keeping their subordinates on an intermittent reinforcement schedule, but they have an intuitive sense that if they alternate punishment (scolding) and reward (praises and raises) and make the moments of reward unpredictable, they will get much more hardworking subordinates who are always keen to show achievements and results.

Another situation I see often has to do with children. A child wants something and is denied by the parent. And then the child makes more noise to show he wants the item. The parent continues to say no. And then the child keeps on raising his pitch and volume until the parent throws up his hands in despair and says, "OK, OK! Just stop crying! I'll give it to you!" *What this does is teach the kid that he will get what he wants only when he cries at maximum volume.*

Sometimes the parent really says no and means it, and the child does not get what he wants. This puts the child on an intermittent reinforcement schedule. He knows he has to scream to get what he wants, but he is uncertain about when he will be rewarded, so he screams all the time for everything he wants.

I've seen kids physically abuse their parents when they ask for the things they want. They go about smashing things and crying at the top of their voices. The parents simply look on in bewilderment and frustration, with a sense that they are helpless to do anything about it. In their hearts they might wonder, "Why do other parents get good kids and I am so *unlucky* to get such naughty ones?"

What behaviorists will say to do is "extinguish" the behavior by removing the reward or by punishing the behavior. By "punishing," they mean a negative consequence to the behavior, like when my parents used to beat the crap out of me when I was out of line.

Being educated in psychology, I used the removal-of-reward method with my own children. When my older son was two years old, he started acting up and insisting that he wanted things his way. He learned to shout and cry until he got what he wanted. So one time, I decided to extinguish this behavior of his and took him into his room while he was crying and asking for something. He cried louder and louder (i.e., his lever-pressing behavior became frantic), thinking that it would eventually result in him getting what he wanted. I just kept repeating quietly but firmly, "No." After about one hour, he got so tired from crying that he fell asleep.

The next time a similar event occurred, I took him to his room again and told him quietly but firmly, "No." He cried for fifteen minutes and then asked nicely if he could go out to play. The third time it happened and I took him into his room and said no firmly, he didn't cry at all. He understood that when Daddy said no, he meant no. So his hysterical behavior was extinguished.

Children are made for crying. It doesn't hurt them in any way to cry. So don't panic when they cry and scream a lot. Focus instead on extinguishing the behavior.

With my second son, who is three years younger, it was easier. When he turned two and started to be loud about what he wanted, he also got taken into the room. But younger brothers tend to look up to their older brothers. When my older son told him, "Just listen to Daddy. When he says no, he means no," he was able to accept it, and he didn't have to go through the extended crying in the room with me.

SCIENCE

Gambling is habitual behavior that is reinforced by psychological conditioning. Casino gambling is a negative-odds situation where you will lose with mathematical certainty over the long run. Stories of winning at casinos are biased, and it stems from people's need to project themselves as winners.

CONCLUSION

There is no such thing as someone having better or worse gambling luck. In the long run, the odds will always play out.

If you are hooked on gambling, you should know that it is because you have been put in an intermittent reinforcement schedule that makes you constantly seek the emotional high of winning.

Despite the problems associated with gambling, you should learn to gamble a little in order to understand odds and risk-taking.

There is no such thing as gambling luck.
Three thumbs down.

LOTTERY LUCK

*I despise the Lottery. There's less chance of you
becoming a millionaire than there is of getting
hit on the head by a passing asteroid.*

—BRIAN MAY

MY MOTHER HAD a visit from a sparrow in the balcony of her apartment, and it proceeded to build a nest in one of her plants. So she called a friend to ask about the corresponding lottery number to buy.

That might seem like an odd thing to most people in the world, but this is how it works in Singapore: We have a lottery system called the 4D. There are four numbers to buy, so you have a one-in-ten-thousand chance of winning the top prize. As there is a total of twenty-three prizes, the odds of winning at least one prize are 0.23 percent per draw. There is a total of twelve draws a month, so if you buy the same number for every draw in the month, your odds of winning at least one prize in a month increase to 2.76 percent. This means that if you keep buying the same number, you are likely to hit at least one prize every thirty-six months or so.

As with any lottery system, there is a lot of superstition associated with it. People will say the lottery owners have entered into supernatural agreements with the gods or demons to ensure they always win. Some will say the system is rigged one way or another or that the payouts change according to the operator's whims. None of these conjectures is true. It all comes down to basic odds. For the Singapore 4D system, every number has a one-in-ten-thousand chance of coming out as the

170

first-prize number. In a "fair odds" situation, you should be paid $10,000 for every dollar you bet on the first prize. But in the 4D system, the payout is only $3,000.

Applying the law of large numbers, what this means is that with ten thousand bets of one dollar from all over the country, there should be one number that hits the first prize. So the operator will have collected $10,000 from the ten thousand bets and paid out only $3,000. This is tilted heavily in favor of the lottery operator. That is why it always wins. There is no supernatural force helping the operator.

But the superstition is there, and there are businesses that have emerged that cater to the superstition. There are 4D apps, 4D analysis tools, books on how to enhance your 4D luck, and the one that my mum's friend had—the encyclopedia of occurrences in life that predict the appearance of numbers in the draw.

Five thousand situations are described in this book, and each situation offers two sets of 4D numbers. Just about all the situations you can imagine in life are described in the book. The nesting of a sparrow, the losing of one's wallet or keys, blackouts, car accidents, getting a fine, finding money—these are all signals for a person to play the lottery. I must commend the author of this book, because it is beautifully illustrated and has detailed instructions on how to interpret the situations in life and find the right number. The book sells very well too. Lots of people who gamble regularly in 4D own the book. As my mother is only a casual punter who does it for fun, she doesn't own a copy, so she had to consult her friend. Her friend checked the book and gave her the number.

So my mother bought the number that corresponded with the nesting of the sparrow in her home, and the number *actually came out* in the next draw, and my mother won $600!

WHAT HAPPENED?

The above story is true; it absolutely happened to my mum. And it's a great story! It is so extraordinary that it is hard to believe it is random chance. There must be some profound explanation for why it happened. So people concoct stories of gods, fate, karma, and ancestor blessings.

But what it was, was just coincidence. It was pure, absolute, unadulterated, dumbass luck!

There are many situations of pure dumbass luck that happen. You walk through a shopping center or airport and just happen to be the millionth visitor that year, and you win thousands of dollars in prizes. You go to your company's annual dinner and dance, and you win the first prize in the lucky draw that sends you to Europe for twenty-one days.

There is absolutely no way to enhance your luck in winning these things. Basically, the event and prizes were created, and *somebody* had to win the prizes! It may look amazing when someone wins it, but it shouldn't. If nobody won the prizes, *that* would be the unusual thing, and people would call for investigations, because there could be a scam. But if the prizes are there, some people will win them.

For years after that win, my mother was visited by cats and dogs and had many other situations that the book says portend the appearance of certain numbers in the lottery. But those numbers did not appear.

For the believers in the book, they will not accept that the book is inaccurate. Rather, they find reasons for why the numbers did not come out. They say it is because the situation that happened did not happen exactly the way the book said it should. They say other luck factors clashed with the situation to render it impotent. *It is confirmation bias.* The believers will just accept the information that confirms their belief. They will not accept any other interpretation.

There are, of course, gamblers who don't believe in the book but believe in other ways through which winning numbers are whispered to them. There are those who say they prayed for the number and that their God told them that a certain number would come out. There are those who say their ancestors appeared to them in a dream and told them about the number. There are those who specialize in buying the license plates of cars that have been involved in accidents because they say that after a misfortune, fortune usually follows. Every 4D punter has their way of thinking that fate, God, or their ancestors are especially blessing them and telling them the numbers to buy.

But it's just the odds, and the odds always play out. The odds predict that some punters will win, but the overall winner will be the operator.

CLUSTERING ILLUSION

I find that the lotteries that allow the players to choose their numbers are the most successful in drawing players. Those that involve the player simply picking a ticket or those that are "scratch and win" are not so effective. In Singapore, other than the 4D, we have the Toto system, which allows punters to choose numbers from one to forty-nine. This is similar to the Powerball system in America, where punters choose numbers from one to sixty-nine.

When the winning numbers come out, the punters can always see some patterns from the numbers or draw some special meaning from them. For example, in the 4D system, if the winning number is 2288, it might seem as though the people who bought 2298, 8823, and 2818, as well as other similar numbers or numbers nearly in sequential order, were "very close." They may feel like they just missed by one number.

For those who play the Powerball or Toto systems, the numbers that come out can have some special meaning to them. "Oh, that number is the last two digits of my good friend's mobile number." "Oh, that was our son's registration number when he started kindergarten." "Oh, that's the house number of our cousin." "Oh, that was our flight number on our last holiday." "That was the license plate of the car that was hit last week." Because we have so many numbers in our lives, the likelihood that winning numbers have some resemblance with the numbers around us is very high. We can always assign some clear or obscure connection to the numbers in our lives if we look hard enough.

This makes the punters feel like the numbers close to them are often winning numbers and that they are *almost* getting it right and that the big win is around the corner. The psychologists call this a clustering illusion. We see patterns and meaning in things that have no connection whatsoever. *There is no reason why the cousin's house number should be a winning number,* but people see it and assign meaning to it.

This keeps them giving money to these lottery systems.

MASSIVE GAMBLE

In the previous chapter on gambling luck, I said that people selectively tell others when they win, and they keep quiet when they lose. It is the same thing with lotteries. You may hear of someone winning at lotteries all the time, and it may seem like that person is very lucky, but in reality, what is likely happening is that the person *buys a lot*, thereby increasing his chances and hence instances of winning.

Likewise, you may have heard of people who always win in lucky draws, and when you look at your own life, you may think you are not very lucky because you have never won in a lucky draw before. But if you get a chance, you should ask the person how many lucky draws he participates in. It is likely to be a very large number.

So it is possible to win, especially for the small lotteries where there are frequent but small payouts. All you have to do is *massively increase your participation*. But in the end, how much will you have spent versus how much you will have gotten in winnings? You are likely to record a loss because the odds predict so. It may not seem like it because your bets are spread out over time, and you are earning an income every month to help pay for the habit. If you total it all up, though, you will have spent a lot of money. If you factor in your effort and time, the costs will be much, much higher.

What else could you have done with all that money and time?

INFORMATION MANIPULATION

The owners of the lotteries like to run advertisements and public relations campaigns to feature the winners of their lotteries. When you read the stories, you will see that the winners are very normal people with normal challenges—middle-class, struggling with finances, going to school, and so on. The stories will talk about how winning the lottery came at just the right time because it helped with an urgent financial predicament.

The purpose of those campaigns is to put in your mind the idea that people just like you are winning. *Why not you?* It's a subtle sell. It's not that there is anything inaccurate about it. But of course, the winners will be the average Joes. The rich and famous don't play lotteries, and the poor can't afford it. So it is the large middle-class people who are all struggling with some financial challenges that buy it.

The lottery companies still make a profit after their massive payouts to the winners, so you can imagine the number of families who lost money to fund the large payouts to the winners, the expenses of the lottery companies, and the large profits that they make.

YOU HAVE GIVEN UP

The *most* troubling reason for you to buy lottery tickets is that *you feel trapped in your current circumstances and that there is no other way for you to improve your life.* Buying the lottery numbs you to the pain you are feeling about your life and gives you a small level of comfort and hope that relief may be on the way. You see life this way: "If I buy, I have some hope. If I don't buy, I have no hope at all."

It is OK to feel helpless. We all feel it once in a while. But if you spend the energy and money you have on the lottery, it will all go to waste. Instead, if you use it to meet people, to learn new skills, and to participate in something creative outside of work, and you are alert to opportunities around you, you may discover new ways of improving your life situation.

Playing the lottery is like an opiate that gives you temporary relief. It gives you false hope.

IF YOU DO STRIKE THE LOTTERY BIG TIME, YOU ARE IN FOR WORSE LUCK

Just google "people who win the lottery," and you will read many stories of people who regret winning it. Their lives often end up in misery, loss, or even tragedy. Imagine you are the lottery winner. Here are the key problems you will face:

You feel even poorer. You may have won $2 million, and before you won that amount, it seemed like a huge figure that could solve all your problems. But after you've won it, you realize it is not enough for all the things you want. You look at people with better lifestyles (and there will always be people who live better than you, regardless of how much you have), and you want more.

You become overconfident. If you're the type who has spent all your time and energy on lotteries, you are likely not to be the type who has developed the necessary skills to manage and grow your money well. When you win a lottery and everyone becomes very nice to you, your ego will be inflated, and you will think you have suddenly become more intelligent and skilled than you are. But that is false confidence bolstered by the people around you who want your money. *Why would you suddenly have the skills when you have done nothing to learn them?* Eventually, you will take risks that you don't understand, like starting a new business or investing in some strange venture, and you will lose money.

When you start to lose your money, you will go back to the lottery because that was what got you the money in the first place, and you will think, "If I can win it once, I can win it again," and you bet more and more until you lose it all.

The money messes up all the relationships. If you don't buy anything for your friends and relatives, they will say bad things about you. If you do, they will not be happy with what they get. They will think about the amount you won and the value of the thing they are getting and think you are a cheapskate. If you do buy something nice, they will come to expect it and turn on you when they don't get more of it.

It's different if you have earned the money. They will not feel they have a claim to what you earned. But since you won it in a lottery, why are you so cheap about it? There have been stories of people who were so harassed by their friends and family for money that they ended up in divorce, substance abuse, and suicide.

Crime. From basic thievery and robbery to sophisticated scams concocted by friends and associates, stories abound of lottery winners, or even insurance claimants, who have lost their money to criminal actions and dodgy schemes from "friends."

SCIENCE

Lotteries are negative-odds situations where there is mathematical certainty you will lose in the long run. They are distractions that give false hope of a better life.

CONCLUSION

I do participate in the lottery once in a while. It's the same with gambling. I do it for fun, like when there's a family gathering and everyone shares in the tickets.

If you ever hit it big because of your casual lottery buying, the best thing you can do is hire a financial planner you can trust to work out a plan so the money will last. It depends on how much you hit, but you shouldn't be surprised that you still need to exercise a lot of discipline in how you spend the money if you want it to last.

Know that the gods aren't smiling at you. You just got lucky with some pure dumbass luck. You have not suddenly become better, smarter, or more of a winner in any way than before you won the lottery. You should be cautious that danger is right around the corner, and you should not make quick decisions about the money. In fact, you should put all the money in a bank, not do anything for at least six months, and work on a plan. That should allow all the swirling madness around you to calm down and for you to create a sensible plan.

There is no such thing as lottery luck.
Five thumbs down.

THE ZODIAC

<hr>

*We are born at a given moment, in a given place
and, like vintage years of wine, we have the qualities
of the year and of the season of which we are born.
Astrology does not lay claim to anything more.*

—CARL JUNG

DOES YOUR ASTROLOGICAL sign have an impact on your life? Let's first talk about what the zodiac is, and then we can discuss what scientific evidence there is that suggests the month you are born in may have an impact on your life.

WESTERN ASTROLOGY

This is based on the position of the sun and stars. The Western astrologists divide a year into twelve periods based on where the sun's position is in relation to the constellations of stars. These periods are spread across the year, so you can check your birthdate and discover the zodiac sign you belong to.

Western astrologists believe that people who are born under different constellations have different characteristics, talents, and idiosyncrasies. Horoscopes are published in many places that give predictions about the future for all the various zodiac signs.

CHINESE ASTROLOGY

The Chinese zodiac is a bit more complicated. First, there is a twelve-year cycle, with different animals representing the years. This is the one everybody is familiar with because it features prominently during the Chinese New Year celebrations.

But if you visit a Chinese astrologer or fortune-teller, he is likely to ask you about the month, day, and time that you were born as well. This is because the month corresponds with the "inner animals" (your character), the day corresponds with the "true animals" (the true you), and the hours correspond with the "secret animals" (what you are secretly).

So a person might be a tiger by year, ox by inner nature, monkey in true nature, and horse in secret nature.

WHY DOES IT SEEM LIKE THERE'S A LOT OF TRUTH IN THE HOROSCOPE DESCRIPTIONS AND PREDICTIONS?

It's because they use generic descriptions that can apply to anyone.

For example, this is my horoscope this year. One statement says, "If you are not careful with your money, there is a danger that you might lose a lot this year." This may sound like an intelligent prediction, but really, if you think about it, it can apply to anyone. Would a person from another zodiac sign *not* need to be careful with his or her money? Would the horoscope say, "This year, you don't need to be careful with your money because no matter what you do, you will not lose any"?

Here's another one: "You have a conflict with the roads this year. Be careful when crossing them. If not, you may meet with an accident." It's a perfect statement. If I don't meet with an accident, it is because I was careful. If I do meet with an accident, well, my horoscope predicted that I would. Here are a few more examples of generic statements. They can apply to anyone.

"There is some travel in your life this year, which might bring about connections with new friends." What does "connections" mean? You're bound to chat with some people on a holiday.

"There might be some disagreements with your boss, which may result in unpleasantness at the workplace." There might be, or there might not be.

"Expect to work harder this year, but there might be some good luck at the end of the year." If the good luck doesn't materialize, it is because you didn't work hard enough.

"Females should not have too much close contact with male colleagues, for such contact may lead to misunderstanding and cause family conflict." That's only for your zodiac sign. For people of other zodiac signs, this would be OK.

"To relieve pressure when you are upset, do some exercise, such as going for a walk with family or friends. And pay attention to your diet by eating more fruit and vegetables." Again, only for your zodiac sign. People from other zodiac signs, please do other things to relieve pressure.

The language leaves a lot of room for interpretation. When believers read them, they project their own life situations onto the statements, and then their minds become primed to the events described, and they go on to become self-fulfilling prophecies.

PSYCHOLOGICAL DESCRIPTIONS

A well-crafted horoscope description should be a statement that sounds like it is unique to the reader when he or she reads it but, in fact, can be applied to just about anyone. For example, "You can be very friendly, but people do not know that you also have a quiet side. Sometimes you prefer to take the hurt in a situation to yourself rather than let the matter become something bigger. You can be self-sacrificial for the people that you love. You are also capable of great empathy for others."

I really just wrote the above passage, like right now, as I'm writing this. If you had read it in the context of a horoscope, you might would think, "Whoa, that absolutely describes me!" But really, *it describes just about everyone.* Everyone thinks of themselves that way. All of us are friendly with quiet sides. All of us prefer to "take the hurt" sometimes. All of us would remember sacrifices we made for our loved ones! What's more, the "Sometimes" and the "You can be" give a lot of wiggle room. People will interpret those terms according to their own life situations.

SCIENTIFIC EVIDENCE ON BIRTH SEASON

Having debunked horoscopes, let's look at the scientific evidence regarding the month you are born and the impact it has on you. Recently, a study that attempted to link birth month to temperament was performed by Semmelweis University in Budapest, and it found the following:

- People born in the summer were more likely to have mood swings between sad and cheerful moods.
- People born in the spring and summer tended to be excessively positive.
- Those born in winter had less irritable moods.
- Those born in autumn had a lower tendency to experience depressive moods.

The amount of research on this is still very light. If there's any link at all, researchers suggest maternal effects, food availability during pregnancy, and sunlight exposure as possible reasons for the different moods or mood-susceptibility that the children may have.

It is a well-documented fact that our moods change with the seasons. So perhaps the mood of the parents or the other caregivers in the first few months of the babies' births might have had an effect on them.

Perhaps.

RELATIVE AGE

Malcolm Gladwell's book *Outliers: The Story of Success* has highlighted the issue of relative age in professional sports players. The data is quite clear that the distribution of players born in the first part of the year is inordinately represented.

The reason could be that as early as the preschool and elementary school periods, the children who were born in the earlier part of the year, who would be more developed physically and mentally than those born in the later part of the year, were selected more for sports activities. Having gained entry into the school's programs for sports, they were given more opportunities for training and development and were hence more able to make it to professional levels of performance.

There is also some evidence that children who are born in the earlier part of the year have a slight advantage in academia over those born in the later part of the year.

These advantages can have important impacts on the personalities of the children on dimensions such as confidence and self-esteem.

SCIENCE

Do you know why people say that babies are brought by storks? It's because storks in Europe would appear around March to nest. A lot of babies would also be born in March because nine months before, in June, the Europeans would celebrate the summer solstice, which was a popular holiday for marriage and fertility.

So the Europeans would see the two phenomena every March, and the storytellers, among them Hans Christian Andersen, would write stories to say that the babies are brought by the storks. But, of course, that is not true. The storks and the babies appearing together is known as a correlation. There is some relationship between the two things—in this case, when lots of babies are born in Europe in March, you can expect to see some storks in the sky—but just because they appear together, you cannot say for sure what the relationship is. You cannot say that one caused the other unless you have more definitive evidence.

Another good example is the relationship between drinking beer and having a beer belly. For years, many people thought it was the beer, but research has now confirmed it is the oily snacks beer drinkers like to eat when they drink beer that gives them the belly.

So the idea that the position of the stars is related to a person's personality could at best be a correlational effect. The actual scientific reasons could be that babies who are born in certain parts of the year exhibit similar characteristics and personality traits because of the weather, the moods of the parents, the chemical activity in the mother at the time of birth (that may be influenced by the weather), as well as the socialization effects from the preferential treatment of the children who are born in the earlier part of the year.

CONCLUSION

Carl Jung was a Swiss psychiatrist who practiced from the late 1800s to the mid-1900s and the quote at the top of this chapter is by him. I think the quote is fair, that we have the qualities of the year that we were born, not because of the stars, but because of the conditions and the seasons of the time.

Even so, my assessment is that any impact there might be is slight, and they should reduce in importance as we age and mature. So the zodiac is mostly psychological trickery. As with all other superstition, people who believe in the zodiac are subject to confirmation bias. They believe in it, and because of their belief, they see evidence of the zodiac's accuracy.

Your zodiac does not affect you or your luck.
Two thumbs down.

YIN-YANG

Remember that sometimes not getting what
you want is a wonderful stroke of luck.

—*Dalai Lama*

THIS IS THE yin-yang symbol. If you google it, you get pretty deep statements that make you want to click away immediately. It is closely associated with the Taoist religion and, along with it, much of the mysticism
the religion has.

But I'm going to avoid the mysticism. I think that whoever drew this
graphic five thousand years ago had a unique understanding of life,

which can give us an insight into *how changing situations can create luck for us.*

Basically, there is black and white, and they make up the whole. And in black there is white, and in white there is black. You cannot just pay attention to the one and ignore the other. It's all a part of reality. In each part, there is the element of the other, so much so that when one part is dominant, *it actually sows the seeds for the opposite part.* And that opposite part will grow until it is dominant. When it is sufficiently dominant, it will sow the seeds for its own decline and for its opposite part to grow again.

BUSINESS CYCLES

I think if there is one thing the yin-yang symbol is designed for, it's the business cycles.

Imagine that you are the CEO of a large chair company, and you read in an authoritative industry report that in the next year, the demand for chairs is going to grow 40 percent. You are about to go to your board to present your plans for next year, and you know that everyone in your board has read about the 40 percent growth projection. What would your projection for your own sales be?

Think about it for a while. Would it be 40 percent, more than 40 percent, or less?

If you said 40 percent or less, you wouldn't last long as the CEO because the board would be wondering why they hired a CEO who would grow the business only by the amount that the industry grows, or less! Any ordinary manager should be able to do that. So most CEOs end up projecting a number that is higher than what the market needs. All the CEOs will think they have clever strategies that will take market share away from the competition so they can sell more than the projected 40 percent growth. This will cause the industry to produce more than the projected 40 percent growth in chair demand.

Now, let's say the market actually did better than the industry report, and the growth of the chair market was greater than 40 percent, so much so that everyone got to sell their extra chairs. In the following year, the industry report may say that growth is expected at 50 percent, which would lead to CEOs projecting sales numbers greater than that. This huge growth in the chair industry would attract many new manufacturers to enter the business because there would seem to be a lot of money to be made. This would cause even more chairs to be manufactured.

At some point, the demand for chairs would start to cool when people had purchased all the chairs they needed. At that time, many of the chair manufacturers would end up with too many chairs that they could not sell. They would then have to slash their prices and maybe even sell at a loss to clear their inventory. This downtrend might persist for a few years. All the companies in the industry would try as best as they could to survive, but as sales dried up, companies that did not manage their business well would declare bankruptcy and exit the industry.

Let's say that after a few years of declining sales, you are due to go back to your board with another projection. The industry report says that demand for chairs is likely to *decline* by 10 percent next year. What would your projection be?

After a few years of barely surviving, you and your board may be battle-scarred and a lot less gung ho. If you say that you project your sales to also be down by 10 percent, your board might be quite happy to accept that projection. They may even advise you to be conservative and plan for lower sales so that you are not stuck with inventory you cannot sell. The whole industry will behave like this, and the amount of chairs made will fall drastically.

Meanwhile, consumers are wearing out their chairs and need replacements. The population is also growing, so more people need chairs. With a low number of chairs being made and with growing demand, there will come a year where there will be a shortfall. With a shortage, chair prices will rise. The increase in demand and price will make chair manufacturers excited again, and you'll be asked to make aggressive projections once more.

And the whole cycle repeats itself.

Growth in the chair market causes overproduction, which leads to too many chairs, which leads to the big reduction of prices, which causes companies to go bankrupt and exit the industry, which causes the number of chairs being manufactured to drop drastically, which causes a shortfall, which leads to prices going up, which leads to more chairs being made, which attracts new manufacturers into the industry, which leads to overproduction again.

This is the market cycle, and it is an important reason for why the stock markets go into these boom and bust periods. The yin-yang graphic explains this perfectly. The boom market sows the seeds for its own decline, but after a few years of decline, the seed is sown for growth to come back again, and it does. If you know how to invest, you will know how to take advantage of these cycles and make money.

AMERICAN POLITICS

There are two main political parties in the United States, the Democrats and the Republicans, which creates a nice yin-yang reality.

The current president, Donald Trump, is from the Republican Party. Before him was Barack Obama, who is a Democrat. Before Obama was George W. Bush, who is a Republican. Before him was Bill Clinton, who is a Democrat.

When the Democrats are too strong with their liberal policies, it creates a reaction in the conservativeness of American voters, and they vote Republican. And when the policies become too conservative, the liberal senses of Americans are agitated again. So the cycle repeats itself.

PARENTING

As I am writing this, we have news that celebrity chef Gordon Ramsay has said that he will not give "a single penny" of his money, some GBP 113 million worth, to his children. Despite earning GBP 43 million in

2016, he gives his eldest daughter, Megan, only GBP 100 a week at university and the other children GBP 50 a week. They have to pay for their own phone subscriptions and bus fares with this money.

Bill Gates is another rich man who has said he will not give money to his children. In fact, he has pledged to give away 99 percent of his money to charitable causes through the Bill and Melinda Gates Foundation. Bill Gates told the Daily Mail newspaper on 1 June 2011 that "'I don't think that amount of money would be good for them…it will mean they have to find their own way,"

Billionaire investor Warren Buffett is also leaving little to his kids. He told *Fortune* magazine on 29 September 1986 that the amount he will leave is "enough money so that they would feel they could do anything, but not so much that they could do nothing."

Shark Tank investor and self-made millionaire Kevin O'Leary is even more extreme. He says he is not giving his kids any of his wealth. He told Chatelaine magazine on 13 Feb 2013, "You want to prepare your children for launching their own lives. I tell wealthy parents that if they don't kick their kids out of the house and put them under the stresses of the real world, they will fail to launch."

Are these parents right to deny their children the luck they were born into? From a yin-yang point of view, their actions are right. These men built their wealth from very little. They managed to turn their poverty into riches. But in riches, they have to be mindful that they are *not* sowing the seeds for poverty again. If they give their children everything they want and their children do not work hard to acquire the skills to manage their money well, and instead think their money will last forever, they will eventually lose what they have.

These self-made men know the value of a purpose-driven life. They know they need to let their children exercise their creative energy toward doing something they feel is meaningful in their lives. If they had so much money that they never needed to do anything for themselves, they might would find life to be meaningless and end up leading destructive lives. We constantly read of children of rich people doing stupid things with their money because they have no sense of accountability and no sense of what their lives' purpose should be.

When rich parents give their children everything, they sow the seeds of misery and failure in their children. Their children will lose a lot of it, if not all. However, the failure of the children may lead to the grand-children having to work harder and acquire the skills to do well in life, so the cycle could turn again.

Mindful of yin-yang reversals, the rich men mentioned above are wise not to give too much to their children.

PERSONAL SUCCESS AND FAILURE

We've all heard that failure is the mother of success. But the opposite is also true: that success is the mother of failure. With an experience of success, a person may become proud and overconfident and blind to his own weaknesses. He may decide to take on projects greater than he can handle. He may underestimate the competition and the amount of resources necessary to properly carry the project out. These issues will cause the person to experience a failure, and he will be humbled. If he is able to pick himself up and try again with honest Positive Energy, he may learn from his failure and achieve success. That's yin-yang happen-ing on the personal level.

Since failure sows the seeds for success, it shouldn't be viewed nega-tively. Success and failure are all part of the whole, and a person needs failure to appreciate success.

Note that after a failure, only the *seeds* of success are sown. If you give up and don't try again, then there is no success, only failure.

STRATEGIES

Once you are aware of yin yang thinking, you will notice many more instances of yin yang cycles. When a country has been peaceful for too long, the people could yearn for action and war. After it's been at war for some time, the people will again yearn for peace. A simple man yearns for riches, and after he has attained riches and the troubles that come with it, he yearns again for a simple life. A woman who has had a few exciting and turbulent relationships may look for a quiet man to be with. After some time, she may again yearn for excitement.

With yin yang awareness, you can better plan your path. When you succeed, you need to be careful rather than proud. You need to manage your success, or else the seeds of failure will grow.

With yin yang thinking, you know that any state doesn't stay forever. Look out for the opposite forces, and watch for them as they grow. Observe the forces as they rise and fall. You can act on the opposite force, if you think it is the right time for it to rise, and benefit from it. Or you can do nothing at all, and just wait for things to trend towards you.

SCIENCE

There is no science here, but an observation that many things in life tend to move in cycles. An ancient philosopher in China noticed it and drew the graphic of the yin yang to convey it.

CONCLUSION

You will notice that I didn't even bother to explain what yin and yang are. There is no need to. Just think of them as black and white, two opposites that are both part of reality and the cause and effect of each other.

The concept of yin and yang is a useful way to see the world. With yin yang awareness you can spot luck and opportunities as they emerge, and avoid failure and losses.

You can plan for the turning of the tides with yin-yang thinking.
Two thumbs up.

LUCKY HUNCHES

Never ignore a gut feeling, but never believe that it's enough.

—ROBERT HELLER

EVERYONE SAYS YOU should trust your lucky hunches, so that's what you have to do, right?

Wrong!

There are certain conditions under which you can and should do so, but otherwise, you should take a thoughtful approach toward decision making. This is because we are very prone to making cognitive errors and jumping to wrong conclusions.

Here are the cognitive errors we often make. There are many more than these, so if you are interested, you can google them, but here are the more common ones.

COGNITIVE ERRORS AND BIASES

Confirmation bias. This was already described in the chapter "Lucky Charms and Jinxes." Our beliefs help us live our lives and make sense of the world. That's why they have a very powerful hold on us. We do not easily let go of our beliefs. So we tend to seek evidence that supports our beliefs. If a belief is challenged with contrary evidence, we are likely to give other explanations for the evidence that support our beliefs or simply reject the evidence as false. For example, if you are a strong supporter of a political party and evidence is presented that your party has made a decision that has adverse effects for the people, your first instinct will likely be to defend your party and explain why the decision might still be right *in the long term* or how it has been deliberately misrepresented by the other party or the press. You might completely ignore good things the other party does or explain them in a way that shows those things to be bad.

Another example is a parent who believes only good things about his or her child and shuts out all evidence that the child is misbehaving or committing crimes. The first response from the parent is, "You are wrong. My son cannot possibly do that." This bias can be called other names. For example, it can be framed as an availability bias. The parent rejects any accusations of wrongdoing by the child simply because he or she has never personally seen the child do anything of the sort.

Saliency bias. Our beliefs and worldviews are constantly shaped by what we read in the press and what is shared on social media by our friends and others. So the prominence (or salience) of the types of news we read shapes our instincts. For example, when we read that a truck has rammed into some people, our instinct is, "Oh, another terrorist attack." Or after the release of a spate of shark movies, if we read about someone dying on the beach, our immediate reaction might be, "Were there sharks?"

Priming. In the movie *Focus*, the character played by Will Smith asks the character played by B. D. Wong to pick a random number and says he (the Will Smith character) will guess it and wager a large bet on it. Of course, he turns out to be right. After all, he is the hero of the movie. But then he goes on to explain that he and his team have been secretly priming the B. D. Wong character the entire day with the number by placing it in the elevators, posters, and songs that he would come across. That's why he had a special affinity for the number and chose it.

The study of priming is a very big area in psychology, sociology, and media. There are many ways with which the brain can be primed to feel or think one way or another. For example, if I want you to think of someone as a doctor, I could plan a visit for you to the hospital in the morning, and then later in the afternoon, I introduce you to someone wearing a lab coat. Your instinct would be to assume that the person I introduced was a doctor, and I can manipulate that to my advantage.

Halo effect. We tend to believe people who are taller and better looking. It's even better if they are celebrities. In their presence, our gut would tell us to accept whatever they said.

Authority fallacy. This is similar to the halo effect. If I introduced you to a university professor, you might readily accept what he or she says. We tend to accept what people in authority say rather than look critically at what they are saying and decide for ourselves.

Genetic fallacy. This is when we give extra credence to someone simply because he or she is the offspring of someone important or who is known for a certain skill. For example, if a person said that he is the son of a chef, we would instinctively think that he has decent cooking skills as well. A negative instance is when we hear that someone is the son of a criminal. We instinctively become more guarded, and our gut will tell us to make decisions that exclude him from positions of trust.

Stereotypes. This is more pervasive than many of us would like to admit. Very often, we jump to conclusions about people because of stereotypes. We have gender stereotypes, racial and cultural stereotypes, tribal stereotypes (e.g., we think all high school students behave a certain way, all biker gangs are the same, etc.), and sexual stereotypes (e.g., a tomboyish girl must be a lesbian).

Suppose you are in a mathematics competition and you have entered the finals. It is then revealed to you by the organizers that you can have one more teammate, and you have a choice of two people you've never met before. You are given their resumes, and you can see that both are equally qualified. But one of them is from South America and the other one from China, who would you pick? With the available information, it would not matter who you picked, but your gut might tell you to pick the Asian because Asians are known to be good at math. This is making a decision based on a stereotype.

Survivorship bias. I've heard people say many times, "My gut told me to buy this stock." I'm not saying the gut does not help in making important decisions, but sometimes there is a survivorship bias when people tell stories of their victories and forget instances of their failures. Research has shown that this is a coping mechanism that helps us get through life, that we devote more of our memories to good things and less to bad. But these stories tend to exaggerate the role the gut plays. In my experience, people who trust their gut in buying stocks will end up losing more money than they make. Stock investment is generally not a gut-trusting thing. It involves research, analysis, and technical ability. When someone says, "My gut told me," it could really be the effects of priming or saliency.

Another example is when someone gambles at the casino and says that his gut tells him to bet all his money on red at the roulette table. When he gets it right, he will go on and tell all his friends about it, saying how he trusted his gut and it proved to be right. When he gets it wrong, he keeps quiet, because who wants to tell the story of how he trusted his gut and got it wrong? So there is survivorship bias here. Only winning stories about the gut get told.

But there is no gut to be trusted in a casino setting. There is no way, whether consciously or unconsciously, that the mind or the gut is able to predict whether red or black comes next. If the color comes out, it will be pure coincidence.

Another situation I am familiar with is when successful people are asked to speak at a seminar. There's always some variation of the "I trusted my gut" story. There is also survivorship bias here because a lot of other people may have also trusted their guts and failed. Those would not have been invited to speak at seminars, so they would not have the opportunity to say, "Don't just trust your gut!"

Groupthink. We all would like to believe we are independent thinkers. But many studies have shown that often we simply go with the group. Sometimes we do it because we don't really have a strong viewpoint. But studies have shown that even if we do have a strong viewpoint that runs counter to the group, we are likely to be influenced by the number of people in the group.

A lot of stories like to say that the person who disagrees with the group is often right and should have gone with his gut to speak up. But this is a kind of survivorship bias because only the stories where a person was eventually found to be right against a group are told.

In reality, most of the time, the group is likely to be formed of intelligent and well-meaning people who make the right decisions. *The fact that they sometimes fall into groupthink and arrive at the wrong decisions should not discount the fact that they more often make the right decisions than the wrong ones.* That's why it makes perfect sense for individuals within a group to suppress their disagreements or feelings of unease if they cannot be sure their disagreements have validity.

<u>Irrational fear or phobias.</u> There is always good old-fashioned fear. Fear is a very useful response because it saves us from danger. And there are a lot of times when we should listen to our guts when it screams "fear" (see below). But there are also a lot of times when our fears are irrational. For example, we can perceive harm when there isn't any, such as walking in the dark in our own homes. Being afraid in the dark is a primal response that saved our ancestors from all kinds of dangers, so we still have that response built into our DNA. But often, we need to let our rational minds take over and assess if there could be any real danger. If we can be sure there is no likelihood of danger, we should carry on with whatever it is we need to do.

WHEN SHOULD WE TRUST OUR GUTS?

When we are prone to making so many cognitive errors and biases, when should we trust our guts? Why do people even say that?

OK, first, let's talk about what the gut is. In physical terms, the gut is part of the enteric nervous system of the body, and it is filled with the same neurotransmitters as the brain. So much so that researchers refer to it informally as "the second brain." According to the researchers, this second brain is able to record experiences and respond to emotions.

Second, let's describe what trusting the gut, *and knowing that it is right*, feels like. American author and psychiatrist Judith Orloff says that most gut instincts are accompanied by physical sensations. She says that positive instincts give:

> *A feeling of comforting familiarity or brightness, you may sense you've known the person before, as with the experience of deja-vu*
> *You breathe easier, chest and shoulders are relaxed, gut is calm*
> *You find yourself leaning forward, not defensively crossing your arms or edging away to keep a distance*
> *Your heart opens; you feel safe, peaceful, energized, expansive, or alive*
> *You're at ease with a person's touch, whether a handshake, hug, or during intimacy*

Negative instincts give:

> *A sick feeling in the pit of your stomach or increased stomach acid, which may prompt an unpalatable deja-vu*
> *Your skin starts crawling, you're jumpy, instinctively withdraw if touched*
> *Shoulder muscles are in knots, chest area or throat constricts; you notice aggravated aches or pains*
> *The hair on the back of your neck creepily stands on end*
> *A sense of malaise, darkness, pressure, agitation, or being drained*

Now, let's look at some of life's situations and see if we can get these feelings.

<u>Big life decisions.</u> In the chapter called "What Do You Want Luck For," I said that it is important that you know what you want to do with your life so you can focus your energy and know how to recognize lucky encounters when they occur. I also offered some ways to think about how to discover what you want to do with your life. I said that you should find something that combines what you like with what you

are innately good at. When you have done all your analysis and met all the people you can meet and you are finally ready to make an important decision about your career, you can check the list of feelings above. If you get the positive feelings, you should be making the right decision.

It's the same when you are marrying someone. If you have the negative feelings, you might want to reconsider.

<u>Expertise.</u> Let's say you are a novice stock investor. If you keep on buying stocks because your gut tells you to, you are going to lose money. You are likely to follow the herd and do all the wrong things. You will panic and sell when the market goes into a sell-down, and you will become irrationally euphoric and buy when the market goes up. So you will end up buying high and selling low.

It's different when you are an expert stock investor. You'd know to ignore the "noise" the market generates and look at what really matters. There will be moments when the data looks a certain way and your gut tells you that something is happening you need to act on. You may not be able to articulate the reasons immediately, but your subconscious is already prodding you to act. It might be a profitable decision to listen to that voice.

What's different with experts is that they've spent a good part of their lives studying their subject matter, and they know it through and through. At the spur of the moment, the assessment of their gut could be important signals.

<u>Danger.</u> In *The Thirty-Six Stratagems*, written by various Chinese militarists through the ages, the thirty-sixth stratagem says that the best stratagem is to run. Sometimes we meet someone and know in our gut that he or she is trouble. We should not be worried about courtesy or political correctness; we should just run. We should not insult that person verbally or say anything to alert him or her to our unease. We should just simply, quickly, and quietly walk, run, or drive away. We could leave the person feeling mystified or even insulted, but better that than risking

danger. The fear might turn out to be irrational, but worry about that later. When you get a sense of danger, run first.

Goodness. Just as we can sense that some people are trouble or pose a danger to us, we can sense goodness in people. There is Positive Energy emanating from them, and we feel comfortable in their presence. When our gut senses someone we've met is good, we should try to spend more time with that person. Good luck, in one form or another, could be around the corner.

SCIENCE

In the very short term, the gut as our second brain gives us a quick assessment of the situations we are in to help us decide on our immediate responses. But this is prone to biases and errors.

In the long term, as we get to know more about the situations we are in, our gut acts as a subconscious check on the decisions we make. If both our thoughtful conscious minds and our reactive subconscious minds are aligned, we should pursue the course of action we have decided on. If they are not aligned, we should rethink.

CONCLUSION

For me, I'd listen to the guts of experts but not novices. They are intelligent guesses, and in the absence of relevant information that can give me greater certainty, intelligent guesses are good enough for me.

For decisions affecting my life, I always have to feel comfortable with them. It should feel like a load has been lifted from me when I make the decision. If I still feel heavy and burdened, I will think I haven't made the right decision and reconsider.

For all decisions, it's important to apply a rational approach where possible. We have to get all the information we can get, reason through the logic, and arrive at something that is the best of what we know at that moment in time. Only then do we check with our gut. If it is peaceful, it's a go.

We should not simply just go with our gut all the time without doing the necessary homework. We are likely to end up making many wrong decisions that will lead our lives through numerous unlucky turns.

Do all the homework you can do, and think things through.
Then go with your gut.
Three thumbs up.

PART V

LUCK SKILLS

ATTACK LUCK

Ninety percent of selling is conviction,
and 10 percent is persuasion.

—SHIV KHERA

So you are sitting next to someone who could give you your big lucky break, and you have the right idea, and the timing for it is excellent. It seems like all the stars are aligned. What do you do? If you freeze and keep quiet, the moment may pass, and the stars may go out of alignment, and it may never come back.

That's why it's important that you know how to sell yourself and your idea. You won't have that skill from out of nowhere; it takes a lot of practice before you can do it well, so you should practice selling until it is a part of your nature.

WHAT IS THE "ASK"?

If you think you need to sell an idea in a short time and that this is a do-or-die situation that's never coming back, you might have a heart attack.

Relax.

If you feel panicky, it means your subconscious knows your odds of success are not high. That's because your "ask" may be too high. This means that you don't know the person you are about to present to well enough, and you are going to ask for something that is very high in value. Those kinds of situations create a lot of anxiety.

There are two things you can do: you can either get to know the person until it feels natural to ask for the big investment, or you can *lower your ask* to something that is easy for him to say yes to. For example, suppose you had a chance meeting with the big boss at the company retreat and you want him to support you in a project that needs a lot more money than what you have in your budget. If you think, "I need to convince him to give me that extra $10 million right now," you are going to burst a blood vessel right there and then. Instead, if all you want is a personal meeting after the retreat, you won't feel so stressed because it is *a smaller ask*.

If you think further and you are still stressed about that personal meeting with your boss because it would be one-on-one, you can lower the ask still, until you feel comfortable. For example, instead of asking for time to present the idea, you should just ask for time to do something the boss likes. For example, if you know the boss likes to shoot pool or that he volunteers at a local charity, you can ask to join him the next time he goes. This is a much lower ask, which should make you feel more comfortable.

After a few occasions of volunteering at the local charity and you have gotten to know your boss better, you can *up the ask* and ask for that one-on-one meeting. At the meeting, if you feel your boss is open to the idea, you can try to close it and say, "I need ten million dollars." If you don't feel your boss is ready to say yes, you can stop yourself and, instead of the $10 million, ask for feedback and advice. Based on his feedback, you can refine your idea and find another opportunity to talk to him later on.

GETTING YESES AND THE EXPOSURE EFFECT

By lowering the ask, you are making it easy for your boss to say yes. You are also in a more relaxed state. People can sense when you are stressed and tensed, and they are more likely to avoid you and decline whatever you are asking for when you are in that state. You have a better chance of getting a yes if you are relaxed and comfortable.

By lowering the ask and getting more opportunities to meet your boss, you allow two things to happen: One, you are using the exposure effect to your advantage. I've explained elsewhere in this book that simple exposure will increase your familiarity and liking for something or someone. The more you know your boss and the more he or she knows you, the likelier you are to like and trust each other, so it makes it easier for you to work on bigger ideas together.

Two, you are getting positive responses from your boss. By lowering the ask and making it easy for your boss to say yes, you are in fact *training him or her to say yes* to you. After a while, your boss will simply find you agreeable and approve the ideas you propose. Conversely, if your ask is too high and your boss says no to you once, it increases the likelihood that he or she will say no to you again in the future.

It's the same if you are asking for a date. If you ask for it out of the blue, it will be very scary. If you are anxious, it will not come out well. You can lower the ask and say, "Hey, can I get help with something I am working on?" This makes it easy for the person you are interested in to say yes, and then you can get to know each other better first and let the exposure effect take over. When you feel comfortable, you can increase your ask and comfortably ask for that date.

TALK ABOUT THE SITUATION

When you finally do get that meeting, what will you say? It's no use talking about your idea immediately; you need to first explain the context. If you have done your research and you are able to paint the need for your idea well, you won't even need to explain your idea. It will be very obvious what the right thing to do is. For example, let's say your company makes pens, and your idea is to make a pen with a titanium nib that can withstand multiple drops and that comes in a steel-alloy casing that is resistant to scratches. You also want to offer it in champagne pink and azure blue. You don't go into your boss's office and talk about this idea. Instead, you present the situation.

This is what you should say: "Boss, our research shows that twelve percent of the pen market in our country, representing $3.5 billion in size, is disappointed by the fragility of the nib. Our focus group members tell us that if they drop any of their pens just once, the nib is gone and they have to buy a new one. This is the key reason why they are resistant to buying an expensive pen. Also, they say that the pen bodies tend to scratch easily and will look dull and unimpressive after a year. This makes their initial investment in any expensive pen not worthwhile."

You've explained the need. You can go on to talk about your idea, but there really is no need to. Your boss might say, "Hey, you know what, we should make a nib out of titanium so that it doesn't spoil, and we should use the new steel-alloy tech from our machines division to make the pen's body."

When you've painted the situation well, the idea is obvious.

As for the colors, that's a detail your boss might not be interested in. Once you get the project, it is up to you to decide on the colors the consumers most want. That's a trick in sales. Once you've closed it, you don't need to oversell it. You don't want to complicate the sale. For example, what if your boss likes your main idea but objects to azure blue? You would have complicated the presentation with a peripheral issue.

TALK ABOUT THE BENEFITS AND WHAT YOU NEED

Once your boss has bought into the idea, you still have to talk about the benefits for the company and for him or her personally. For example, you may say, "We can launch this new product in a year, and that would add an additional thirty million dollars to our sales next year and five million in net profit. I'm looking at our corporate targets for next year, and I think this would be the growth our board is looking at." Your boss may already be thinking about his or her bonus when saying, "Great, so what do you need?"

At the top, I talked about how you need to lower the ask if you are not sure. This is not what you do when you have sold the idea. This is your big break, and you need to show your abilities. Don't chicken out with a low ask. Say, "Boss, to do this right, I need an additional ten million dollars to my budget for this year." Your boss may say, "Whoa, that'll burst our overall company budget."

At which point you remind him or her of the benefits by saying, "It would pay for itself in two year, and the stream of profits thereafter would help the company meet its future growth expectation." So now your boss is not just thinking about next year's bonus but the next *few* years' bonuses.

THE EMOTIONAL SELL

You have to be clear about what it is your client wants. (Here I use the word "client" to mean anybody you are selling to. In the example above, your client would have been your boss.) And it is not always clear what he or she wants.

When I was working in P&G, my clients were large retail chains. I found that it was useful to use psychologist David McClelland's Three Needs Theory to classify my clients. He says that human beings have three needs in the workplace: achievement, power, and affiliation. People with the achievement need want to show results so they can get ahead in the company. People with the affiliation need do not want to get ahead. They are content where they are and just want to be friends with everyone. People with a power need are likely to be more senior people who need power associations to get ahead. They are less interested in achievement and more interested in getting to know powerful people.

I had all three types as my clients, so I sold to them accordingly. For the achievement-oriented clients, I talked about market share, sales, and profit. For the affiliation-motivated clients, I took them out for lunches and became their friend. There was nothing I could do about the power-motivated clients because I was young and junior. When I needed something important done with these clients, I had to drag my bosses down to meet with them. I would still be the one to do the presentation and close the sale, because they were my clients, but my bosses needed to be in the same room, or else I wouldn't even get a chance to present.

As I moved on to sell other things, I met clients with other types of motivations. Some had tremendous ego needs, so I had to say things that met their egos, like "I was at this meeting, and I heard these guys talking about you! They couldn't believe their luck that they have you as their partner!" I met clients who were very high in their empathy quotient, so I'd say, "I was thinking we could set aside a part of the profits that we make for charity." The list goes on. There are clients who are insecure, those who love to take big risks, and those who need something to be aesthetically pleasing before they will participate.

There's a lot in motivational research that you should read up on and learn so you know how to appeal to the right motivations of your clients and close the deals.

THE RIGHT TIMING

There is a Chinese saying that when the following elements align, you have to strike:

1. The right timing
2. The right place
3. The right people

When you have all these things, your lucky break has arrived. It would be such a waste if you didn't know what to do with it. Learn to sell, and practice constantly until it becomes a part of you. You'll need it to attack the luck when it comes.

Capture the luck when it comes by learning to sell.

DEFEND AND DEFLECT

*We can't control our world but we can
control our reactions to it.*

—*Susan Jeffers*

WHAT IF YOU are working in an environment that is full of negativity and your boss is always on your case? You might feel very stressed and confused. You have to try to take control of your own situation. You do this by choosing how you respond to the interactions with your bosses and your colleagues. The principle is to be "problem focused" while maintaining Positive Energy. It's hard to do in the beginning, but as you start to acquire this skill, you will feel so much more in control of your life.

Here's how you do it.

BE PROBLEM FOCUSED.

Suppose your boss came to you and said, "You are the stupidest manager I have! You can never get things right! This is lousy work!" How would you respond? Instinctively, you might feel like lashing out and cursing your boss's mother and three generations of his relatives, but here are other possibilities:

- A: "If you're so damn clever, why don't you do it yourself?"
- B: "Hey, don't get yourself so worked up. You're going to burst a vein. Tell me what's bugging you."

- C: "Are you always this mad with your employees?"
- D: "I'm very concerned that you said that. Please show me where I have gone wrong, and I will correct it."
- E: "Erm, I have a very urgent appointment with a customer. Can I come back to you on that?"
- F: "I'm sorry, I'm sorry, I'm sorry, I'm sorry…"

Which one should you choose? The moment you pick an option, you understand you have a choice. You *can choose* how you respond.

But you ask, "Which one is the right answer?" I'd say that *it depends on the outcome you want.* If you have just been offered a new job by a better company and you are so pissed off with your current boss that you cannot take it anymore, you can choose A. I wouldn't recommend it because you still want to leave on good terms with your ex-boss, and you never know how things can change in the future.

If you are the type who answered F, then you are totally controlled by your environment. In this case, you are controlled by your boss. When he comes out and scolds you like that, your self-esteem and confidence are destroyed. If you have been doing this, stop. There are other responses. B and E don't solve the problem. C may be disrespectful and patronizing, which will make matters worse.

I recommend D. Here you are problem focused. You ignore all the emotions and focus on fixing the problem and getting the job done. Let's see how the conversation can continue with D.

You: "I'm very concerned that you said that. Please show me where I have gone wrong and I will correct it."
Boss: "I don't know why I'm paying you. You're absolutely good for nothing!"
You: "If I have done something wrong recently, please let me know so that I can fix it."
Boss: "Fix it? You don't know how to fix yourself a sandwich!"

You: (silent, deciding to let your boss let it out.)

Boss: "I knew I would lose money the day I hired you!"

You: (silent)

Boss: "Look at this report that you wrote. The comparison dates are wrong, and the data is incomplete! High school students write better than this!"

Aha! The problem. You should hear more of it before you answer.

You: "So, the comparison dates and the data, I see. Is there anything else?"

Boss: "Anything else? You better be damned happy that there is nothing else! If there were something else, you wouldn't be sitting there still."

OK, so you have isolated the problem.

You: "Could you be more specific about what is wrong with the report so that I might correct it?"

Boss: "Are you deaf or plain stupid? I just said the dates are wrong; the data is incomplete."

You: "Hmm, I see the problem with the dates. I can get it amended straightaway. How is the data incomplete? What else would you like me to add in there?"

Boss: "Anybody with some sense will know that with a report like this, you have to include three years' worth of numbers so that an accurate comparison can be made."

You: "I see. Will there be anything else?"

Boss: "No, that's all, you twit!"

You: "I can have these to you by two p.m. Thanks for bringing the improvement areas to my attention."

That's how you take control. You should realize that any emotional confrontation at the workplace usually has a practical problem as its source, so you should focus on finding out what this problem is and finding a solution for it. I don't mean to discount the emotions. They are real, and you should take note of them. But don't react to them and let your own emotions rule you. You will only create more emotional responses that are hard to manage.

Remember the very first chapter about the most important thing in luck? You don't project Negative Energy, ever. Don't complain to anyone about your boss. Don't vent on the Internet. Continue to smile and focus on adding value. Keep doing that, and you will change everyone around you in the manner that they respond to you. They will know you are full of good energy that's directed toward solutions, and they will relate with you that way.

YOU HAVE BETTER CONTROL THAN YOU THINK

I know some people will read the above exchange and think they would not have that kind of control of their emotions. But I tell you that you can.

Let's talk first about controlling emotions. Do you think your emotions are instinctive and your personality is fixed and you just respond accordingly? That's a misconception. While we are born with certain predispositions and we are generally of a certain personality type, our personalities are evolving all the time, and we change as we age and experience new things. Our control of our emotions gets better and better with time.

Now I'm going to show you the kind of control you have over your emotions.

Can you cause yourself to feel hunger right at this very moment? Yes, you can. You can think of all the yummy food you love, and you will salivate, and your stomach will automatically create the hunger hormone to tell you to go eat the thing you want. Can you now think of something nauseating and lose your appetite? Yes, you can. Think of someone you don't like, and think of doing disgusting things with him or her; did you lose your appetite and hunger pangs? Can you think of something and be angry? Can you think of something funny and laugh and feel happy? Can you think and feel horny?

You can, you can, you can. This is you influencing your body and your emotions with your thoughts.

STOP! RECHANNEL!

This is a trick I learned when I was young. When I am feeling sad or angry, I ask myself this question: "What is the outcome I want?" Where is this sadness or anger leading me? If it's leading me down a path that will help me achieve the outcome I want, then I let it continue. If it doesn't, I say out loud, "Stop! Rechannel!" And then I redirect my mind toward the outcome I want and focus on the solution. Or I think about something else completely.

You can try it. Say out loud to yourself, "Stop! Rechannel!" And then latch on to another thought. It's not so easy to learn this technique initially, but as with anything, if you practice, you will get good at it over time.

The trick is to ask, "What will I accomplish if I continue on this emotional track?" If the answer is nothing, you will find it easier to rechannel. Do not let emotions you know are unproductive or destructive fester in your mind. Do not give energy to those emotions.

WE ARE EMOTIONAL CREATURES

Emotions are a kind of intelligence that helps us cope with life. For example, if you feel uncomfortable about something, it's your body telling you something is not right and that you should run, avoid, or refuse. Another example is depression. There is limited research to show that depression is actually a coping response for when we are overwhelmed with something. It makes us antisocial and withdraw into ourselves so our conscious and unconscious minds can work out how to deal with the challenging thing that just happened.

When we are shouted at, like in my example with the boss above, our bodies turn on the "fight or flight" hormones, and we feel anxious and stressed. Most people will want to relieve this as soon as possible either by finding a quick excuse to run away or to lash back and engage in a full-on "fight" response.

The problem-focused approach I recommend is a kind of "managed fight." You are not running way but engaging with your boss in a controlled manner. It is a tough but effective coping response. Your insides will be exploding to want to fight or run, but you are managing it to assert personal control. Our emotions are primitive response systems, so we need to have control over them so we can manage our lives.

Having made that point, however, I must say it is not so easy to undo millennia of conditioning. It's already in our DNA, so we should not be in too much of a hurry to "manage our emotions away"! If you feel like you want to stay away from people just a few days more to deal with your emotions, you should do so. You are not wallowing or admitting defeat. You are just allowing your subconscious mind more time to deal with the situation.

But be aware that at some point soon, you have to make the decision to stop. If you don't, there is the danger that your negative emotions will pair with something positive, such as tremendous support from a loved one, and your mind will start to think there is a reward for negative emotions. After that, your mind might choose responses that are filled with drama in order to get the positive reward of emotional support from your friends and loved ones.

LEAVE NEGATIVE ENERGY ENVIRONMENTS

Although I say you can defend against Negative Energy, sometimes the best way to change your luck is to change environments. I know I said that luck takes time and that patience and perseverance are needed. But that's true only if you are operating in a Positive Energy environment. If you are operating in a Negative Energy environment full of drama and angst, and everybody is more concerned about seeking satisfaction for their own emotions than on getting things done, nothing good will happen, no matter how much patience you put in.

So there are techniques to defend, but if they don't change the situation, you have to decide if you should move on. Too much Negative Energy can be bad not just for your career health but your mental and physical health as well. It's exhausting to be defending all the time.

TECHNIQUES

These two chapters have been focused on techniques. In the previous chapter, I describe the selling skills you need to have to attack luck when it comes. Here, the focus is on managing the Negative Energy that is all around you. You have to be the shining example of Positive Energy amid all the drama that is played out at work. You don't want to be lost in all that drama and waste energy and emotional resources grappling with it.

With these techniques, you will stand out as the person who gets things done, and you will make it amenable for good luck to find you.

Defend against bad luck by focusing on solving the problem.

CONCLUSION: THE RECIPE FOR LUCK

*Those who have succeeded at anything and don't
mention luck are kidding themselves.*

—LARRY KING

LIFE IS A journey of luck.

We had no influence over the genes we were born with and the circumstances we were born into. The schools we went to, and the friends we made there, were also largely a consequence of where we lived or decided for us by our parents. When we finished school, the economic situation of the world and the country we live in, which largely determined the opportunities available to us, were also not of our doing. Finally, how, when and where we die are also not up to us.

Somewhere along the line, we develop our own identity and we determine for ourselves the direction that our lives take. Those are rare and precious moments when we take charge of our lives and drive it in a direction that fulfills us. But as we embark on the journey that those decisions take us, we find yet again that many things are beyond our control.

I feel it is important that we first have the awareness of the role that luck plays in life. We are then able to think about developing skills to manage the unexpected events as they come, and to live our lives in a way that would attract more positive events than negative ones.

217

THE RECIPE FOR LUCK

Thanks for staying through to the end! I hope my sharing has been beneficial, and you have gained important insights into life and luck. Here's a quick review of the ideas in this book. I have worded and arranged it slightly differently from what's in the book so it's easier to read.

THE "RECIPE" FOR GREAT LUCK

1. Start by thinking of yourself as lucky.
2. Decide what you would like to accomplish with your life.
3. Put Positive Energy behind it.
4. Learn and experience new things.
5. Turn up at events and engage deeply with Positive Energy people.
6. Be appreciative of the luck you are born with and develop it.
7. Keep on top of important global trends.
8. Learn to invest.
9. Learn to gamble and take some risks.
10. Exercise and take care of your body.
11. Declutter your life from unnecessary drama and stuff.
12. Be patient.
13. Be brave.

Lucky 13!

Here is the summary on how to deal with age-old superstitions about luck.

1. Many of the "luck" superstitions may be true observations about human behavior but just explained the wrong way.
2. Keep lucky charms. Why not? If they make you feel powerful, by all means.
3. Feng shui is environmental psychology. Optimize your work environment for peak performance.

4. Karma thinking is important. Do good for good to come back to you.
5. Learn to pray deeply. You connect with your spiritual self and strengthen your will.
6. Stop compulsive gambling.
7. Stop buying lottery tickets.
8. Don't waste time on the zodiac.
9. Be aware of yin-yang thinking to capitalize on reversals.
10. Do your homework, and then trust your gut.

And I shared with you two skills that would be useful to manage luck.

1. Learn to sell.
2. Learn to manage your emotions and responses.

When you do the things listed above, good luck will happen. It's not superstition. It's mathematical, and it's psychological.

I've shared many stories from the viewpoint of an entrepreneur and investor. I feel that is a great vantage point from which to look at luck because I meet lots of people with lots of energy who are working hard on their ideas and battling with luck every day. Some encounter good luck and some don't, and I've been able to see why.

I've tried to share the social science of luck wherever possible in the book. But the human race has not mapped out all the science about human behavior yet, so I have tried to share some insights through stories, experiences, and logical arguments.

I've enjoyed writing this book! I think it is tremendous luck that we live in the age of information. We can free ourselves from the superstitions associated with luck and think of it in scientific and logical terms.

I wish for you an amazing life with great ideas, great people, and great opportunities coming at you in many different ways.

Great luck to you!

ABOUT THE AUTHOR

MOH HON MENG is a seasoned Internet entrepreneur who cofounded iFAST Corporation, an Asian-centered securities brokerage firm listed on the Singapore Stock Exchange. He is also the cofounder of Fundsupermart.com, ShareTransport.sg, and TheRightU.com, and has invested in other Singapore-based online ventures.

Hon Meng graduated from the National University of Singapore in 1992, where he studied economics, psychology, and philosophy. He has written novels, plays, and self-help books aimed at the Singapore market.

Hon Meng is married and resides in Singapore. He has two teenage sons.

END NOTES

The Most Important Thing about Luck: Positive Energy

1. "A new form of energy may have powered the Big Bang". *Universe Forum*. Accessed 29 May 2017.
   https://www.cfa.harvard.edu/seuforum/bb_whatpowered.htm

2. Thomas C. Corley, "In 5 years of studying rich people, I learned they make their own luck — here's how you can make yours", *BusinessInsider* website, 13 Feb 2016. Accessed 1 June 2016.
   http://www.businessinsider.sg/how-rich-people-make-their-own-luck-2016-2/#iPAKVI56KoudFFo3.97

3. Thomas C. Corley, "I spent 5 years studying rich people, and here's what they tend to have in common". *BusinessInsider* website, 9 March 2016. Accessed 1 June 2016
   http://www.businessinsider.sg/things-rich-people-have-in-common-2016-3/#8UGssH6GvyCP6piE.97

What Do You Want Luck For?

4. "Steve Jobs' 2005 Stanford Commencement Address". Youtube: Uploaded on Mar 7, 2008, accessed 1 June 2017.
   https://www.youtube.com/watch?v=UF8uR6Z6KLc

5. "Steven Speilberg's Advice". Youtube. Uploaded on Apr 5, 2011, accessed 1 June 2017.
   https://www.youtube.com/watch?v=kBN9jpooZoM

6. Mihaly Csikszentmihalyi, "Flow" *TED Talk*. Youtube: Uploaded on 4 Oct 2015, accessed 1 June 2017.
   https://www.youtube.com/watch?v=I_u-Eh3h7Mo

Where Does Luck Come From: Part I—Ideas

7. "Steve Jobs' 2005 Stanford Commencement Address". Youtube: Uploaded on 7 Mar 2008, accessed 1 June 2017. https://www.youtube.com/watch?v=UF8uR6Z6KLc

8. Gary Wolf, "The Next Insanely Great Thing". *Wired Magazine*, February 01 1996. https://www.wired.com/1996/02/jobs-2/

Where Does Luck Come From: Part II—People

9. Thomas C. Corley, "In 5 years of studying rich people, I learned they make their own luck — here's how you can make yours", *BusinessInsider* website, 13 Feb 2016. Accessed 1 June 2016. http://www.businessinsider.sg/how-rich-people-make-their-own-luck-2016-2/#iPAKVI56KoudFFo3.97

The Second Most Important Thing about Luck: Belief

10. "What Is the Placebo Effect?" *WebMD* Accessed 1 June 2017 http://www.webmd.com/pain-management/what-is-the-placebo-effect#1

11. Deborah L. Feltz, Sandra E. Short, Philip Sullivan. *Self-efficacy in Sport.* (Published by: Human Kinetics, 2008), Page 169.

12. David E. Conroy, PhD, "Enhancing Motivation in Sport" *Psychological Science Agenda* American Psychological Assocation. February 2006 http://www.apa.org/science/about/psa/2006/02/conroy.aspx

13. Christopher J. Beedie, "Placebo Effects in Competitive Sport: Qualitative Data". *The Journal of Sports Science and Medicine.* Published online 1 Mar 2007. https://www.ncbi.nlm.nih.gov/pmc/articles/PMC3778695/

14. Wilkins, William E., "The Concept of a Self-Fulfilling Prophecy". *Sociology of Education,* published by the American Sociological Association, 1976. 49 (2): 175–183.

15. Maltby, J., Day, L., Gill, P., Colley, A., Wood, A.M. (2008), "Beliefs around luck" Personality and Individual Differences. *Elsevier.com* http://personalpages.manchester.ac.uk/staff/alex.wood/Luck.pdf

The Luck You Were Born With

16. Global Rich List: Accessed 29 May 2017 http://www.globalrichlist.com/

Your Generation's Big Luck

17. Bill Gates, "Dear Class of 2017 …" *Gatesnotes* article. Published May 15, 2017, accessed 1 June 2013. https://www.gatesnotes.com/About-Bill-Gates/Dear-Class-of-2017

Luck Takes Time

18. George Bernard Shaw, play, *Man and Superman,* Published 1903

19. Jack Welch., *Winning,* HarperCollinsPublishers, London 2005, p278-280.

Luck Favors the Brave

20. Thomas C. Corley, "In 5 years of studying rich people, I learned they make their own luck — here's how you can make yours", *BusinessInsider* website, 13 Feb 2016. Accessed 1 June 2016. http://www.businessinsider.sg/how-rich-people-make-their-own-luck-2016-2/#iPAKVI56KoudFFo3.97

Lucky Charms and Jinxes

21. "Professional Profile: Robert Zajonc". *Social Psychology Network* web site. Accessed 1 June 2017.
http://zajonc.socialpsychology.org/

Feng Shui

22. University of British Columbia, "Effect Of Colors: Blue Boosts Creativity, While Red Enhances Attention To Detail." *ScienceDaily.* 6 February 2009.

Karma

23. "Whatever it is life gives to you, remember, you started it." Anonymous. Brainyquote.com.
https://www.brainyquote.com/quotes/keywords/karma.html

Prayer

24. Emma Seppala, Ph.D., "20 Scientific Reasons to Start Meditating Today: New research shows meditation boosts your health, happiness, and success!" *The Science of Happiness, Health and Success.* Website. Accessed 1 June 2017.
http://www.emmaseppala.com/20-scientific-reasons-to-start-meditating-today/#.WS6aeGiGOUl

25. Stephanie Liou, "Meditation and HD". *Huntington's Outreach Project for Education at Stanford.* 26 Jun 2010. Accessed 1 June 2017
http://web.stanford.edu/group/hopes/cgi-bin/hopes_test/meditation-and-hd/

Zodiac

26. Olga Khazan, "How Birth Season Affects Personality:. 22 Oct, 2014. Accessed 1 June 2017.
    https://www.theatlantic.com/health/archive/2014/10/how-birth-season-affects-mood/381727/

Lucky Hunches

27. Judith Orloff, MD., *A Formula For Trusting Your Intuition*. Trans4mind website. Accessed 30 May 2017
    https://trans4mind.com/counterpoint/index-spiritual/orloff.shtml

www.ingramcontent.com/pod-product-compliance
Lightning Source LLC
Chambersburg PA
CBHW061436180526
45170CB00004B/1427